MW00814025

Praise for My Indian Table

From the time I was in medical school in New York, I took great pride in learning how to cook quick and simple meals in 30 minutes or less. Since I was not a great cook, I was particularly attracted to meals with ingredients and instructions that were simple and easy to follow. I have evolved since then as a mom and more importantly as a doctor, understanding better the correlation between what we eat and the state of health that our bodies are in, and not just on how fast I can prepare my meals. I have always loved Indian food because of the spices and the sensory overload associated with them. I have been looking forward to Vandana's My Indian Table for years and am delighted that her years of education and cooking, love for food, and teaching are all combined in this amazing book that demystify Indian cuisine. Her Tofu Bhurji is the excellent complement to my family's big, mostly non-vegan, weekend breakfasts. I surprise myself at how great my dishes come out and how I can tweak each meal because she offers alternative spices and food selections that encourage experimentation. I am particularly fond of curry and garbanzo beans and her Chana Masala is a favorite go-to dish when I am hungry and short on time.

When feeling under the weather, I reach for my Turmeric Milk Latte (with coconut milk) as a great substitute. Her recipes are easy to follow and since each dish comes together so quickly and promotes a predominantly plant-based diet, My Indian Table is the perfect solution to healthy meals for our busy lives. Vandana's passion for cooking and her knowledge of ingredients are not just thrown together; they are combined with a story to tell about the health benefits of her ingredients and how each ingredient, individually and collectively, affect our nutritional core. My Indian Table has brought my love for Indian cuisine and culture into my home and the variations of meals that I can prepare have become endless.

-Carline Louis-Jacques, **MD, MPH**

Vandana Sheth's expertise as a Registered Dietitian/Nutritionist, Certified Diabetes Educator and her zeal for healthy lifestyles that feature plant-based meals for family and friends are evident in these recipes.

Vandana has provided the Indian food lover like myself, easy-to-prepare meals that are packed with a delicious pairing of flavors and healthful, easy-to-find ingredients.

Move over salt, sugar, and ghee; Vandana's home-made meals are here to enjoy!

-Wahida Karmally, **Dr.PH, RDN,CDE,CLS,FNLA**
Special Research Scientist, Columbia University
Associate Editor, *Journal of Clinical Lipidology*

My Indian Table

Quick & Tasty
Vegetarian Recipes

Vandana Sheth, RDN, CDE, FAND
Registered Dietitian Nutritionist & Certified Diabetes Educator

Copyright © 2019 Vandana Sheth

All rights reserved.

No part of this publication may be reproduced, distributed, or transmitted in any form or by any means, including photocopying, recording, or other electronic or mechanical methods, without the prior written permission of the publisher.

ISBN: 978-1-7338153-2-1 (Paperback)
First Edition
First Printing (April 2019)

Disclaimer: This book is based on the author's experience and knowledge and has been written and published for information and educational purposes only. It is not intended as a substitute for care and counsel provided by medical professionals. Please consult your health professional for medical advice. Although every effort has been made to provide accurate and current information, this book cannot guarantee to be free of factual error. The author shall have no liability of any kind for damages of any nature whatsoever caused and will not accept any responsibility for any errors, omissions or misstatements that may exist within this publication.

Photography by Lora Ackermann

Food Styling by Vandana Sheth

Cover and interior design by Mariana Vidakovics De Victor

Printed in the United States of America

Published by Vandana Sheth

Rancho Palos Verdes, CA 90275

www.vandanasheth.com

Acknowledgments

This book is dedicated to my wonderful husband, Rajan, and sons, Rajiv and Vijay, because of the joy, appreciation, and enthusiasm you have always shown me for my home-cooked meals. To my amazing mother, Pravina Chokshi for being such an inspiring role model when it came to family meals and being creative in the kitchen. To my father, Harish Chokshi for always being the wind beneath my wings. My sisters, Heena and Kay, for being my cheerleaders. My parents-in-law Hasu and Bharti Sheth for their unconditional love and guidance. To my wonderful extended family, friends, my teachers and professors who have helped enhance this book in countless ways. To the thousands of clients I have had the honor of helping for pushing me to be more creative in meeting their unique needs with delicious food choices.

Thank you to my wonderful dietitian friends and colleagues who have inspired, encouraged, and supported me through this journey. Special thanks to Ruth Frechman, Sharon Palmer, Constance Brown-Riggs, Wahida Karmally, Gita Patel, Cynthia Sass, Chere Bork, Libby Mills, Carline Louis-Jacques and so many others. Thank you so much, Lora Ackermann, for capturing my story with your beautiful photos and being my flow editor. A special shout-out to my friend Nirav Bhakta for the frequent brainstorming chats about my book.

I am proud to be an American and thankful for my rich Indian cultural heritage, both of which are prominent in my personal and professional lives.

The main purpose of this book is to share my passion for enjoying predominantly plant-based meals that are delicious, easy-to-prepare and Indian-inspired. All the recipes are vegetarian, but can easily be made vegan. Many of the recipes are also gluten free. Research has shown that slowly shifting our food choices to include more plant-based options can have a positive impact on our health and environment. Regardless of whether you are following a vegan, vegetarian, or plant-based diet, recipes in this book will delight your palate and expand your food choices. I invite you to explore the joys of *My Indian Table* and create wonderful food memories gathered around your table. Thank you, readers, for taking this culinary journey with me.

Namaste

Table of Contents

Dedication

This book is dedicated to my wonderful parents, Harish and Pravina, for their unconditional love and support, and to my three "boys," Rajan (husband), Rajiv, and Vijay (sons), for always allowing me to pursue my passions.

Atithi Devo Bhava

This is a beautiful Sanskrit saying which loosely translates to *Guests are like God*.

This symbolizes the hospitality and love shown to anyone who visits an Indian home. I was raised in a home where this philosophy was fully embodied and it has become an integral part of our home today as well.

Foreword

By Sharon Palmer, RDN, MS in Sustainable Food Systems, The Plant-Powered Dietitian

All around the world, healthy people eat healthy, plant-based foods. This is a tradition that dates back through the millennia, as humans in tribes, groups, and societies gathered precious plants to form the backbone of diets that nourished and sustained their kin, promising the survival of the next generation. Over the years, decades, and centuries, people passed down knowledge about life-giving plants. That particular grass produces an exceptionally delicious, energizing grain when cooked. This legume plant produces large, fleshy, nutritious beans in the summer, which can be sun-dried and then packed away to cook during the lean months. This particular shrub produces a pungent leaf that, when dried, adds much needed flavor to stews, but also seems to boost immune function. And that root, when ground, provides rich color and flavor to sautéed dishes and seems to help people grow to reap a rich, long life. Those fruits that fall from the tree taste as sweet as honey, yet also seem to protect the body from disease.

These rich food and nutrition diseases are on full display in the Indian food culture. Steeped in the history, folklore, religion, soil, place, and people, the foods from this land are not only some of the most flavorful and joyous to be found, but some of the most healthful. India boasts the largest percentage of vegetarians in the world. Based on cultural and religious preferences, the cuisine has focused primarily on plants throughout history. And, oh, how lovely those vegetarian dishes are! Slow-simmered dal dishes, brightly colored sauces, piquant chutneys, crunchy, earthy salads, chewy-soft, as well as papery-crisp, breads—such is the stuff of the Indian vegetarian table.

As a plant-based dietitian, I have always advised my clients and community to look to the food ways of India for plant-based inspiration. My favorite entreaty is, "Look to the ethnic foods of India, as they really know how to do plant-based cooking right!" There is no better way to spice up your healthful, plant-based diet than by adding a pinch of aromatic, satisfying Indian food to your weekly menu. As a child growing up in the Pacific Northwest, Indian food was only to be found in a friend's home, as Indian restaurants were not common. When I moved to Southern California and was exposed to the bounty of ethnic foods over the years, I became so accustomed to the flavors of India that they are now a true expression of American comfort food to me. I am surely not alone, given the popularity of Indian foods and flavors in supermarkets and restaurant menus today. My sons will always, hands down, pick our neighborhood Indian restaurant for their birthday dinners.

But sadly, many Indian restaurants don't serve authentic, lovingly prepared, health-promoting Indian food, as my longtime friend and colleague Vandana knows too well. Often, you will dine on rich, cream-laden American approximations of Indian dishes. While they are indeed delicious, it is just the tip of the iceberg in terms of flavor and health! There is a wide world of nuanced, special Indian regional dishes you might not ever encounter, unless you take Vandana's wonderful cookbook into your own kitchen, open the pages, and start trying some of these treasured recipes. While you may fear that Indian cooking is beyond your time constraints and ability, have no fear. Vandana's recipes are easy to prepare, and based on foods that you can find in your own markets. Best of all, she brings her lifelong love and appreciation for the best of Indian cuisine, and her honored career as a respected registered dietitian nutritionist to the table.

Let Vandana introduce you to a more healthful, true version of the most precious of Indian dishes, and let it paint your lifestyle with all of the joy, vibrancy, and health that awaits you. Let your meals become a celebration—colorful, happy, flavorful, and long—as you linger over that last bit of sauce on your plate and munch on that last lemony cucumber in the salad. Let her knowledge fill your mind, body, and soul. Treasure these traditions, which were passed down from her ancestors, that she shares in the pages of this book, and let them inspire a newfound love of Indian vegetarian food. Enjoy the journey!

Eat and Live Well,

Sharon Palmer, RDN, MS in Sustainable Food Systems
The Plant-Powered Dietitian
Author of *The Plant-Powered Diet Series*, and blogger at SharonPalmer.com

Introduction

The sizzling sound of mustard and cumin seeds splattering, the aroma of freshly ground and whole spices, the hissing sound of the pressure cooker releasing steam, and the whirring of the blender--all of these evoke fond childhood memories of my mom's bustling kitchen in Madras (now known as Chennai), India. Every morning, local fruit and vegetable vendors stopped by our home and I would watch my mom make careful selections of seasonal produce that would guide her meal plan for the day. She had a great interest in cooking and was so creative with our meals and snacks. She never really used measuring spoons or cups and intuitively cooked with a wide array of spices and herbs to enhance the flavor of food.

My mom also often used food remedies when we were feeling sick. One example, which you can find in this book, is Rasam, a spicy broth, commonly made and enjoyed with rice. In my family, Rasam was used as the South Indian version of chicken soup here in America. Our enjoyment of food is often associated not just with the taste and flavor of the dish, but is also influenced by our memories associated with the food. My mom has taught me a lot about food, nutrition, and especially the relationship between food and family traditions. Food is so much more than simply fuel for the body. Food connects us in a profound way to one another, to our environment, culture, memories and can bring a lot of joy. As a registered dietitian nutritionist and certified diabetes educator, I love using my science-based knowledge to

transform heavy Indian dishes to healthier options. I have helped thousands of clients over the last two decades prevent and manage various chronic health conditions. I truly believe that traditional Indian foods and spices can promote health and prevent disease.

Indian food is vibrant, flavorful, and varies across the country. My family was originally from the Northwestern state of Gujarat, known for its vegetarian cuisine, and I was raised in the Southern state of Tamilnadu. There is great diversity among Indian food choices across different states in terms of grains, spices, flavors, and cooking methods. I was raised on a delicious blend of Gujarati and South Indian vegetarian food.

When I fell in love with my husband and moved to America in the early 90s, I was surprised at the huge gap between the Indian food I was raised on and popular Indian food served in restaurants here. There is so much more to Indian food than chicken tikka masala, naan, samosa, and vindaloo (not that there's anything wrong with these choices). I was also amazed at how many people would ask me what I ate if I was a vegetarian - only salads? Thus began my passion for sharing my heritage and culture through food. Every time we entertained at our home, or anytime I took food to a party, although I would have a variety of food choices for our friends, the biggest hit was always the Indian vegetarian option. Over the years, friends, colleagues, and clients often asked for my recipes but more importantly encouraged me to write a cookbook. This spurred my desire to write this book, sharing delicious and flavorful Indian recipes that tickle your palate and enhance your health. Recipes in this book are a culmination of some of my mom's recipes, and inspiration from the amazing cooks in my life including my mother-in-law, aunts, friends, and my imagination. Whether you are a meat-lover, vegetarian, or vegan, this cookbook is for you, as it's a flavorfully fun way to enhance your meal options.

If you are overwhelmed or intimidated by the idea of preparing an Indian meal at home, I encourage you to be open. Two common myths associated with those who are unfamiliar with Indian cuisine are that they have to buy a ton of expensive spices and ingredients for just one recipe that they'll never use again, and that Indian cooking takes too long; however, once you invest in a few basic spices, you will be reusing them in varying combinations throughout this book. As a working professional, wife, and mother to two wonderful sons, although I love to cook, I, too, needed to simplify the process and build shortcuts without giving up on flavor and taste. As a result, I have tried to streamline the cooking process in this book to help you prepare.

With this idea of minimizing time in the kitchen and maximizing taste, I have taken shortcuts such as canned beans, canned tomatoes, pre-cut fresh produce, and frozen produce; however, you can certainly create everything from scratch. Regardless of your culinary skill level, I hope you will give this book a try. Have fun along the way with creating your own beautiful memories with simple and delicious Indian food surrounded by your loved ones.

From *my* Indian kitchen, to your table, I truly believe that you can Eat Well Your Way for Life!

Namaste

Eating the Indian Way

Traditionally, Indian food is not served in courses. Various dishes are served all at once at the table, family style. Typically, a vegetarian meal would include rice or bread, one or two vegetable dishes, a bean or lentil dish and possibly plain yogurt. The meal may be served in a stainless-steel plate called a thali, with various components and the liquid dishes served in small bowls. In the south, sometimes banana leaves are used instead of a plate.

Indian food is eaten with your hands and so it is important to wash your hands before you sit down to eat and, of course, afterwards. Generally, the right hand is the only one used to eat while the left is kept on your lap. Rice is mixed with various food items and enjoyed with your hand. If bread (roti/chapati) is served (typically in a North Indian meal), a small piece is torn off and used to scoop or dip in various dishes on the plate. Eating food with your hands may take some practice, so it is okay to use utensils if you need them.

The book has been divided into sections for your ease. If you feel overwhelmed, especially on a weeknight, to attempt making multiple dishes, focus on my 'Light Meals' section for even easier one-dish meal ideas, This section will also make clean-up easy.

I wrote this book to share my love for cooking Indian inspired meals. Most of the recipes can be prepared in 30 minutes, assuming you start with all the ingredients including cooked rice, beans, or lentils. All the recipes I have included are family favorites. They are a compilation of old family recipes and my creativity. Yes, the list of ingredients may seem overwhelming, but know that most of the recipes will use the same ingredients in varying combinations. There are no substitutes for some ingredients like asafetida or curry leaves, and it is okay to skip a few ingredients if you don't have them. All the recipes have a personal connection whether to my childhood home in India or my family home in America. Besides English and Hindi, India has 21 official languages spoken throughout the different states in the country. The Indian names of ingredients and titles of the recipes in this book are either in Hindi, Tamil (Tamil Nadu) or Gujarati (Gujarat). All the measurements in this book are based on U.S. measuring system. One cup = 237 ml or 8 ounces, one teaspoon = 5 ml, one tablespoon = 15 ml. Below you will find additional suggestions for success when using this cookbook.

Here's to savoring many wonderful meals surrounded by your loved ones, from my table to yours!

Suggestions for Success

1. Since all the recipes have been created with the idea of speed, it is important that you first read through the recipe completely. Next, have all the required ingredients prepped, organized, and ready on a counter before you start cooking.

2. Serving sizes may seem on the smaller side -- please adjust according to your preference and desire. Since Indian food is often served with multiple courses, portions listed are smaller.

3. Indian cooking is more an art than a science. Feel free to adjust or make substitutions as desired. Recipes provided can be used as a guideline with room for your creativity.

4. I have tried to include ingredients that are more readily available in America. However, if you are missing an ingredient it is okay to skip it.

5. When buying spices, try to store them in an easily accessible spice container (masala dabba) or in a rack with individual spices nearby.

6. Many of the recipes suggest heating a saucepan or skillet on medium-high heat. If you place your palm above the pan and you can feel the heat, the pan is appropriately heated.

7. When heating oil, it is important that the oil gets hot but not overheated. Use an oil that is capable of handling high heat. I have used canola oil in all my recipes but you are welcome to use any other oil that has a high smoking point especially, when you use it for deep frying.

8. When adding cumin seeds to hot oil, sauté until darker brown, not black. If the oil is too hot or you have left the cumin seeds too long in the hot oil and they turn black, it is best to discard them and start with a fresh batch.

9. When adding mustard seeds to hot oil, they pop and can splatter. Be careful and step back from the stove to avoid accidental splatter onto your skin. If you would like, you can use a splatter screen.

10. In most recipes I have kept red chili or green chili as deseeded and optional. If you prefer less spicy, skip these and if you like it more spicy, keep the seeds and use the chili.

11. A quick note about cilantro. Cilantro is used throughout the book in many recipes as an addition or garnish. However, I know many friends and clients who do not like cilantro. It is absolutely fine to skip it.

12. When you are cooking beans, it is best to add acidic ingredients such as tomato or lime after the beans are cooked as they can prevent beans from tenderizing during the cooking process.

13. When cooking beans or lentils, try to make a double batch so you can use one half and freeze the other portion for a future date.

14. Once you cook plain rice, spread it out over a baking sheet to cool and allow grains to stay fluffy and not stick together before using in recipes such as lemon rice or coconut rice.

15. To make recipes vegan, substitute a plant-based oil or fat for ghee, plant-based yogurt for regular yogurt.

16. To make recipes such as roti and puri (glorious grains section) gluten free, switch whole wheat flour for a gluten-free flour. You may need to play around with the exact portions of flour to water as they work differently. Alternatively, you could simply use a gluten-free tortilla or wrap in place of traditional roti or puri.

Stocking Your Indian Kitchen

Cooking Tools and Equipment

Stocking your kitchen with the right tools can make cooking a lot easier. I have listed some tools that I use. However, you can adjust this list based upon what you may already have at your home.

1. **Pressure Cooker, Instant Pot, Slow Cooker** - Every Indian kitchen owns at least one or more pressure cookers. Any of these would make it much faster to cook beans and lentils from scratch.

2. **Cutting board** - My mom never used a cutting board. She was skilled at chopping things with her fingers while holding a knife in her hands. I never mastered this skill and prefer to use a cutting board. It is important to keep your cutting board clean to avoid food safety issues. Either wash by hand or in the dishwasher to completely sanitize after each use.

3. **Mini-Food Processor or Blender** - Helpful in shredding, pureeing, making dips and sauces

4. **Grater** - Especially useful for shredding vegetables and ginger

5. **Knife** - Depending upon the size you like and are comfortable using for cutting

6. **Peeler** - Useful for peeling carrots, potatoes, etc.

7. **Masala dabba** - A traditional stainless steel Indian spice box with individual bowls for various spices/seeds. You can also simply buy individual spices and store them in a drawer or on a shelf.

8. **Kadai** - An Indian wok. You can also use an Asian wok or deep pot. Typically used for deep frying or stir-frying.

9. **Mortar & Pestle** - you can find them in marble or metal. Helpful for crushing whole spices, ginger, or mincing garlic. As a young child, I remember being assigned the task of peeling cardamom pods and crushing seeds with the mortar and pestle. It was a special time because usually my Mom needed cardamom powder for an Indian sweet treat.

10. **Spice Grinder** - basically a coffee grinder exclusively for grinding spices. This eliminates the need for a mortar and pestle.

11. **Tava** - cast iron rimless skillet. You can also use a low-rim skillet from an American store. This is typically used for roti, Indian style crepes - dosai, or pancakes.

12. **Rolling Pin** - Typically used to roll out dough for roti, puri, paratha. It can also be used to crush seeds and some spices. They come in a variety of materials and thicknesses. Find one that works for you. I use a wooden rolling pin.

13. **Can Opener** - useful especially if you plan to use canned ingredients as mentioned in the recipes such as beans, tomatoes, and tomato sauce.

14. **Cooking Spoons** - I like using wooden or silicone spoons, or a slotted spoon, spatula, or ladle.

15. Measuring cups and spoons

16. 4-quart saucepan (stainless steel or cast iron)

17. 16-quart Stockpot

18. Small Skillet for tempering oil with spices

19. Baking Sheet for roasting vegetables or spices in the oven

20. Sieve/Colander for straining and draining

21. Bowls for making dough, sorting, rinsing, and cleaning rice or beans.

22. Other specialty items you may need for a recipe.

23. **Thali** - stainless steel-rimmed plate may be used to steam and make dhokla. You can also use a round baking tin in place of a thali.

Key Ingredients

Fortunately, with the growing interest and demand for global cuisine, many Indian ingredients can be found in your local grocery store or through online vendors. However, some essential ingredients may still require a quick trip to your local Indian grocery store. I have attempted to limit the number of spices and ingredients so that once you stock up with them, you will be able to use them in multiple recipes throughout the book.

Whole wheat flour - Atta

I have vivid memories of a huge burlap sack made up of jute filled with whole wheat kernels delivered to our home a few times a year. My mom would slowly go through the mountain of kernels to ensure that is was free of rocks/foreign objects, and then send it our local mill to grind into freshly ground whole wheat. This would be stored in large, airtight bins in a cool storage area to be used slowly over the next few months. Now, we can easily purchase whole wheat flour in a ready to go bag. This is used for making homemade flatbread roti, chapati, paratha, puri. At Indian stores, you can find pre-made, rolled chapatis in the refrigerated section that can simply be cooked at home.

Rice

Rice is the predominant grain in south Indian food. Rice plays an important role in Indian culture. It is thought to be a symbol of prosperity, is used as part of some ceremonial rituals, and is used as a baby's first food. There are many varieties of rice available and used in India. Basmati the aromatic, long grain variety is often thought of as the queen of rice. It is available in white, brown and red types. Medium- or short-grain rice is often used for everyday cooking. You can find rice at your local stores raw (needs to be cooked), pre-cooked and shelf-stable (just warm up), and frozen, fully-cooked.

Beans, Lentils, Legumes

Legumes are plants that come in pods and include beans, lentils, peas and peanuts. **Pulses** are part of the legume family but include only the edible seeds inside the pod. Pulses include garbanzo beans, dried peas, lentils and beans. They are an excellent source of protein, fiber, vitamins, minerals and are budget friendly. Legumes and Pulses have been an integral part of Indian cuisine. Most Indian kitchens, including mine in America, have at least 10-15 varieties of pulses and other legumes. I have listed the ones used in this book below.

Garbanzo beans - also known as chickpeas come in two types. The larger round almost pea shaped, yellow bean commonly found in America called kabuli chana in India. The second type is smaller, dark brown in color and called kala chana in India. In my recipes, I have used kabuli chana commonly found in your regular store's dry beans section. You can also find them already prepared in cans and pouches as well.

Kidney beans - Rajma - are dark-red or brown kidney shaped beans. They can be found in your regular stores dry beans section. You can also find them already prepared in cans and pouches as well.

Moong beans - are dark green, oval shaped, small lentils. They may be found in your regular stores dry beans section or certainly at middle-eastern and Indian stores

Black-eyed peas - Chola - also known as cowpeas are small, oval-shaped, light-colored beans with black spots. They can be found in your regular stores dry beans section. You can also find them already prepared in cans and pouches on the shelf as well as fully cooked in vacuum-sealed pouches in your produce section.

Tuvar dal - this is the split and skinned inside of pigeon peas. They look similar to chana dal or even yellow split peas. However, they are not the same. Tuvar dal is smaller in size and tastes different. There are two varieties found in Indian stores - oiled and dry. I prefer to use the dry variety. If you can only find the oiled variety, wash it thoroughly in hot water before using.

Chana dal - Split and de-husked brown garbanzo beans (kala chana) produce bright, yellow lentils. This is ground and used as garbanzo bean flour (besan) in some recipes. Chana dal is cooked as a lentil dish but also added to oil in tempering for added crunch to dishes such as lemon rice, coconut rice, and coconut chutney. Chana dal looks similar to yellow split peas and tuvar dal.

Moong dal - Split and de-husked moong beans produce a pale yellow colored, small lentil. They cook quickly and are used as a dal, cooked along with rice to make khichdi, and in the south Indian dessert sakkarai pongal. You may find this in your local grocery store or certainly at your local Indian store.

Urad dal- Split and de-husked black lentils produce a white, small lentil. In this book, I have used them mainly for tempering in oil for some of the recipes. You will most likely only find this at your local Indian store.

Masoor dal - Split and de-husked red lentils that come from whole red lentils which actually look light brown in color. Split red lentils look vibrant, almost orange in color when raw; interestingly when you cook them they turn yellow. These can be found in your regular grocery store or an Indian store. They cook fast and make for a delicious soup.

Garbanzo Bean Flour - Besan - It is otherwise known as gram flour, chickpea powder/flour, besan. Garbanzo bean flour is high in protein, fiber and naturally gluten free. It is used to make Indian style crepes/pancakes, added to stews as a thickener, used as the base for popular snacks, and sweets.

Spices and herbs are a fundamental component of Indian cuisine. They add an exciting depth of flavor but also add positive health benefits. Herbs are the leaves of plants. Spices can include the bark, buds, roots, fruit, seeds, stem and leaves of the plant. Some plants may provide herbs and spices. For example, coriander seeds (Dhania) is regularly used in its whole or ground form in Indian cooking and the leaves called coriander leaves in India and cilantro in America are regularly used as a garnish or as part of a chutney.

Cumin seeds - Jeera is a small, oval-shaped, brown colored seed. It is a key component of many of the dishes in this book. You can find it at your regular stores or Indian market. It is best to add it to hot oil until it turns a darker brown but not black. You can find ground cumin in the spice aisle of your stores. However, if you want to enhance the flavor and have the time, I suggest you dry roast whole cumin seeds and crush them for your recipes.

Mustard seeds - Rai comes in two varieties - white and dark-brown/black. The dark colored mustard seeds are more commonly used in Indian cooking. They are usually added to the tempering stage with oil in recipes. It is important to remember that mustard seeds do pop and can fly out of the pan when cooking. Don't get too close to avoid getting accidentally hurt. You can find mustard seeds in the spice section of your regular stores and Indian stores.

Coriander seeds - Dhania - are the seeds that produce cilantro or coriander leaves. They are brown colored and round. You can find them whole or ground in the spice section of your stores. I use ground coriander seeds in many of my dishes and it is an important part of my masala dabba (spice box).

Fenugreek - Methi seeds are small, yellowish-brown in color and used in tempering. They are an important ingredient in spice mixes. They provide several health benefits and are added to dals to help offset any stomach discomfort. You can find seeds or ground fenugreek at Indian stores along with fresh fenugreek leaves.

Turmeric - Haldi is a vibrant, golden yellow colored spice that comes from the turmeric root. This is one of the most common spices and always has a spot in Indian spice boxes. It adds a beautiful hue to food but can also stain your hands. Try to wash your hands quickly after handling it to minimize staining. Turmeric powder can be found in the spice section of your grocery stores. You may also find fresh turmeric root in the produce section during certain times of the year. Besides its importance in cooking, turmeric is also used in India as part of many home remedies. Haldi doodh - turmeric milk tea is a common remedy for colds and coughs.

Red chilies - Lal Mirchi are a variety of dried, red chilies that are used whole or ground. Depending upon the spice level you enjoy, you can use this as an optional ingredient. Red chili powder is an important part of most Indian spice boxes. You may substitute paprika for a milder alternative.

Asafetida - Hing is a pungent-smelling powder made from a resin. This is a very common ingredient in Indian cooking and thought to have digestive benefits. Since it has a strong sulfur-like odor, it can mimic the aroma and flavor of onion and garlic. Asafetida is sold in small, airtight containers at Indian stores.

Ginger - Adrak - is a root that adds a unique fragrance and flavor to dishes. You can find fresh ginger root in the produce section of your store. SInce many of the recipes require minced ginger, I often make a big batch and store it in small containers in the refrigerator and freezer for future use. You can also find ground ginger in the spice section of your store and that can be used in some recipes.

Garlic - Lasan - is the root of the plant and adds a strong flavor to food. You can find garlic cloves whole (covered with a papery white skin), peeled in the produce/refrigerated section and minced in jars or in the freezer section of your store. Garlic powder is also an option and is available in the spice section of stores.

Cloves - Laving - are small, wooden pieces with rounded tips that are actually unopened flower buds. They have a distinct aroma and flavor. You can find them whole or ground in the spice section of your store.

Cinnamon - Tuj-are bark from the cinnamon plant and have a strong aroma and flavor. It is used in tempering to add flavor to dishes, in tea as part of masala chai, and roasted/ground in garam masala.

Cardamom - Elaichi - are green colored pods that are aromatic and hold dark colored flavorful seeds inside. To release the seeds, you can use the flat side of a knife to press gently, a rolling pin, or a mortar and pestle. In recipes where you use the whole cardamom pods, I suggest you gently open one end so the fragrance and aroma can add to the dish. When you need just the seeds, save the empty pods to flavor your tea. You may find cardamom at your regular stores or for sure at Indian stores. There is another type of cardamom - larger black pods that have a different flavor and aroma. Most of my recipes use the green cardamom pods.

Black peppercorns - kali mirch or mari - are actually berries that grow on the pepper plant. Black peppercorns have a strong flavor. You will find them whole or ground in your local stores. If you need ground black pepper, I suggest you buy whole ones that go into a peppermill to crush fresh as they release a more intense flavor.

Saffron - Kesar is the one of the most expensive spices in the world. They are thin strands that are the dried, hand-picked stamens of the crocus flower. They add a beautiful orange-yellow color and rich fragrance to food.

Curry leaves - Kariveppilai - these leaves add a unique strong aroma and are very commonly used in south Indian cooking. Since this is hard to find outside of Indian stores, I have not used it in any of my recipes which traditionally would use curry leaves.

Cilantro - Kothmir/dhaniya - are cilantro or coriander leaves that are used in many dishes as a vibrant garnish as well as ingredient in recipes. The stems have an intense flavor and so when able, I often use the stems and leaves.

Cooking oil - I use canola oil in most of my recipes in this book. Canola is a monounsaturated fat that provides omega 3 fats and is stable at high cooking temperature. You are welcome to use other oils per your preference.

Tamarind concentrate or paste - Amli - you can find a jar of readymade tamarind paste or concentrate at an Indian store. Tamarind paste is made from the flesh of tamarind (a brown, pod-shaped fruit of the tamarind tree) and adds a slightly sweet-sour flavor to food.

Shopping and Storage Tips

☼ Most of the ingredients listed in this book can be found easily at your local grocery store, warehouse stores or through online merchants. You will also find a "Little India" shopping area or at least an Indian grocery store in most major cities in America. Visiting one of these stores can be a wonderful and adventurous experience. Depending upon the size of the store, you may find groceries, fresh produce, frozen items, and a cafe. These stores will be more cost-effective in comparison to regular stores. Also, some markets such as Sprouts will allow you to purchase spices through a self-serve process (buy what you need). This can be another cost-effective way of buying spices.

☼ Whole wheat flour should be stored in an airtight container and used within three months or it may start becoming rancid.

☼ Canned beans usually last for one year. Pay attention to the expiration dates and store accordingly in your pantry. Dried beans can last for one to two years in your pantry but they may need more time to soak and cook.

☼ Dried spices should be stored in a dark place in airtight containers to preserve the color and flavors. Whole spices can have a shelf life of four years and ground spices of about two or three years.

☼ Fresh herbs such as cilantro will last longer if you trim the stems and store them in water.

Wine Pairing with Indian Food

Although I did not grow up drinking wine with food when in India, living in California, I have grown to enjoy it.

My husband and I are fortunate to know many wonderful winemakers and enjoy some special wine tasting experiences. So, when it comes to Indian food, what works?

Pairing wine with Indian food can get tricky because of the layered spices and heat. Here are some guidelines--

Enjoy white wines with mild fruity flavors and acidity such as a sauvignon blanc. It pairs well especially with dishes that include tomatoes and citrus notes. Sauvignon blanc may also be refreshing with a rich coconut-sauce based dish.

Dry rosé and sparkling wines can also pair well especially with heavier sauces.

Gewurztraminer and Riesling can pair well with spicy Indian food as the residual sugars may cut through and counter some of the heat.

Red wines that have intense fruit flavors would also work well with the complex Indian flavors

However, it is ultimately all about what tastes good to you. Use the above notes simply as ideas.

Chilled beer, especially light beer, pairs well with Indian food. You may find Indian restaurants serving Indian beers.

Basic Recipes

This section features a few basic recipes that will help you towards your adventures into Indian Vegetarian Cuisine.

Recipes

How to Cook Plain Rice

Ingredients

Makes 4 servings

- 1 cup uncooked white rice (basmati or long-grained)
- 1.5-2 cups water

Method

1. Place rice in a small bowl. Rinse the rice with water while rubbing the grains with your fingers. Drain into a sieve and repeat this process another two or three times.
2. Add drained rice and water into a medium-sized saucepan on high heat. Bring to a boil.
3. Stir, reduce the heat to low and cover the saucepan.
4. Simmer until all the water has been absorbed and you may see tiny shallow holes on the surface indicating water has been absorbed. This takes about 8-10 minutes.
5. Turn off the heat and let the covered saucepan rest for 5 more minutes on the stove.
6. Fluff the rice gently with a fork before serving.

....

Notes

It is important to thoroughly wash rice before cooking to ensure it's clean and to remove the starchy residue. Thoroughly rinsed rice will allow for a less sticky grain. This basic rice recipe is used almost daily in South India. This is the rice I use for most of the rice dishes in the book.

Special Notes about Dried Beans, Lentils and Peas - Legumes

Legumes are notorious for having small pieces of stones, dirt and grit. It is especially important to sort for foreign objects and clean thoroughly before cooking with them.

As a child, one of my kitchen tasks was to help with sorting the beans and lentils.

Method

Here is how you do it--

1. Place the beans or lentils you plan to use on a plate (I typically use a light colored plate or stainless steel plate). Use your fingers to sort through the beans or lentils to remove any dirt, rocks or blemished legumes
2. Place the dried legumes in a bowl and cover with water
3. Use your fingers to rub the legumes while swishing around in the water.
4. Drain the water using a sieve and repeat this process with fresh water another two or three times.

If you plan to make dried beans or peas from scratch, it is best to soak them in water overnight to expand, become tender and speed up the cooking process.

How to Cook Beans From Scratch

Ingredients

- ❁ 1 cup dried beans
- ❁ 4 cups water for cooking + more for cleaning and soaking
- ❁ ¾ teaspoon salt

Method

1. After you have sorted, cleaned and drained your beans, soak them in a large bowl filled with water. Cover and set them aside overnight.
2. Drain the soaked beans into a colander
3. Place the drained beans and water in a large saucepan on high heat and bring to a boil.
4. Reduce the heat to medium-low, cover the saucepan and allow the beans to simmer until soft. This may take about 45 minutes.
5. Drain excess liquid (save it for some recipes), add salt, stir and use as needed

How to Cook Split Lentils - Dal

Ingredients
Makes 4 servings
- 1 cup dal
- 2-3 cups water
- ¾ teaspoon salt

Method
1. Place dal on a plate to sort and remove any dirt
2. Clean well by placing lentils in a bowl filled with water while rubbing with your fingers. Drain and repeat two or three times.
3. Place lentils and water in a medium-large saucepan on high heat. Bring to a boil.
4. Reduce heat to medium, cover the saucepan partially and stir periodically
5. Lentils may take up to 30 minutes to become well cooked and soft
6. Ensure that the water does not boil over during the cooking process.
7. Turn off the heat and use lentils in a variety of ways as shown in the recipes

Dal is the generic term to describe both the raw and cooked version of lentils, split lentils, legumes

How to Make Ghee

Ghee is pure, clarified butter used in cooking as well as playing an important role in religious ceremonies.

Ingredients
- 1 pound unsalted butter

Method
1. Place butter in a heavy saucepan on medium heat until it starts melting
2. Reduce heat to low and simmer for ~15 minutes
3. Stir and remove foam from the surface as it arises
4. Pay close attention to the color - as soon as it reaches a clear golden color with solids settling in the bottom of the saucepan, turn off the heat.
5. Cool slightly, strain through a cheesecloth covered sieve into a jar or container

How to Sprout Moong Beans

Ingredients
Makes 4 servings
- ⚙ 1 cup whole moong beans
- ⚙ 4 cups water for soaking

Equipment
- ⚜ Medium-sized bowl
- ⚜ Colander
- ⚜ Cheesecloth

Note
This process takes anywhere from 1-3 days depending upon how long of a sprout you want.

Method
1. Sort and clean whole moong beans well
2. Soak beans in a bowl with four cups of water overnight
3. The beans will typically double in volume.
4. Line the colander with a cheesecloth and drain the water.
5. Wrap the beans in the cheesecloth and rest the colander in a dark place such as your cold oven or pantry.
6. You will start seeing the bean sprouts in 12-24 hours.
7. Use immediately or store in the refrigerator for up to five days.

Chai Masala

Traditionally, tea is the beverage of choice in North India. Chai is the term for tea and masala simply means spices. There are many variations to the spices added to tea to create unique flavor profiles.

Ingredients
- ¼ cup cardamom
- 2 2" cinnamon sticks
- 3 tablespoons cloves
- 4 tablespoons ginger
- 1.5 tablespoons black peppercorns
- 1 teaspoon ground nutmeg

Method
1. Dry roast whole spices in a pan for 2-4 minutes until you smell the aromatics
2. Cool slightly and crush in a spice blender. Add ground nutmeg and mix.
3. Store in an airtight container and use as needed
4. If you choose to make this even easier, you can use already ground spices. Mix them well and store.

Instant Chai Masala

A quick and simpler version of traditional chai masala

Ingredients
Makes 4 servings
- 1 tablespoon ground ginger
- ½ teaspoon ground cardamom
- ¼ teaspoon ground cloves
- ¼ teaspoon ground nutmeg
- 1.5 teaspoons ground cinnamon

Method
1. Mix all the ingredients in a small jar and store for future use.

Instant Garam Masala

A quick and simpler version of garam masala

Ingredients
- 4 tablespoons ground coriander
- 2 tablespoons ground cumin
- 4 teaspoons black pepper
- 1.5 teaspoons ground cloves
- 1.5 teaspoons ground cinnamon
- 1 teaspoon ground cardamom
- ½ teaspoon ground nutmeg

Method
1. Mix all the ingredients in a small jar and store for future use.

Garam Masala

Literally means "hot" spice mix. This is a key spice mixture used in North Indian cuisine.

Ingredients
- ½ cup cumin seeds
- ¼ cup coriander seeds
- ½ cup cardamom
- ¼ cup black peppercorn
- 3 tablespoons fennel seeds
- 2 tablespoons cloves
- 10 2" cinnamon sticks
- ¼ cup bay leaves
- 1 tablespoon nutmeg powder

Method
1. Heat a skillet on medium high and dry roast all the ingredients except nutmeg powder. Stir continuously and roast for 2-3 minutes
2. Turn off the stove, allow to cool and crush in a mini food processor or spice grinder
3. Store in an airtight container for future use

How to Make Homemade Yogurt

Yogurt is used in multiple ways in Indian cuisine. I have fond memories of my mom making yogurt every night before going to sleep.

Ingredients
- 3 cups nonfat or low fat milk
- 1 tablespoon yogurt starter

Method
1. Heat milk in the microwave or on the stove to a boil
2. Cool until lukewarm (the ideal temperature for bacteria to activate)
3. Add yogurt starter and mix well with a spoon
4. Cover and place on the counter (at room temperature) until the yogurt is set
5. Place the set yogurt inside your refrigerator for future use

Sambar Powder

This spice mix can be made in advance and used as needed when making south Indian dishes such as sambar. It can also be added for additional flavor to vegetable dishes.

Ingredients
- 1 cup coriander seeds
- ¼ cup whole red chili
- ⅓ cup tuvar dal - split pigeon peas
- 2 tablespoons chana dal - split garbanzo beans
- 1 tablespoon urad dal - split and de-husked black gram/lentils
- 1 tablespoon fenugreek seeds
- 1 tablespoon turmeric powder
- 1 teaspoon cumin seeds
- 2 tablespoons whole black peppercorns

Method
1. Dry roast all of the ingredients in a pan on medium-high heat for a few minutes
2. Cool and grind in a spice grinder
3. Store in an airtight jar or container for future use

Instant Sambar Powder

A quick and simpler version of traditional sambar powder

Ingredients
- 3 tablespoons ground coriander
- 1 tablespoon ground cumin seeds
- 1 tablespoon ground tuvar dal
- 1 tablespoon ground fenugreek seeds
- ½ teaspoon ground red chili
- ¾ teaspoon ground turmeric
- ¼ teaspoon black pepper
- ½ teaspoon asafetida

Method
1. Mix all the ingredients well with a spoon or whisk
2. Store in an airtight container for future use

*Fenugreek seeds add a distinct smell and taste to sambar. It can be found in Indian and Middle eastern grocery stores.

Beneficial Beans, Lentils, Legumes

Legumes are plants that come in pods. Pulses are part of the legume family but include only the edible seeds inside the pod. Pulses include garbanzo beans, dried peas, lentils and beans. According to the United Nations Food and Agriculture Organization, there are 11 types of pulses. They are an excellent source of protein, fiber, vitamins, minerals and are also budget friendly. Pulses play an important role in Indian vegetarian cuisine. A typical Indian pantry will have at least 10-15 varieties available for regular use. Most homes would use their pressure cookers to cook either lentils or beans at least once if not twice a day. I have used a combination of five beans and lentils in the recipes.

Recipes

Split Garbanzo Bean Lentils with Mushrooms

Chana Dal with Mushrooms

A delicious split garbanzo bean and vegetable stew. Chana dal is the Indian name for split brown chickpeas. My mom used to make dudhi chana dal (dudhi is the Indian name for a type of squash). I love mushrooms and so my version below is created with spices and mushrooms. Mushrooms are a good source of B vitamins, selenium, vitamin D, high in water content, low in calories and provide a powerful umami flavor.

Ingredients
- ✿ 4 (1 cup) servings
- ✿ 4 cups cooked chana dal
- ✿ 1 teaspoon canola oil
- ✿ 1 teaspoon whole cloves
- ✿ 1 cup diced onions
- ✿ 1 cup diced fresh or canned tomatoes
- ✿ 2 cups chopped mushrooms
- ✿ ½ teaspoon ground coriander
- ✿ ½ teaspoon ground cumin
- ✿ 1 teaspoon ground turmeric
- ✿ ½-1 teaspoon garam masala
- ✿ ½ teaspoon ground red chili (optional)
- ✿ 1 teaspoon salt
- ✿ 1 teaspoon lime juice
- ✿ 2 tablespoons finely chopped cilantro

Method
1. Sort, clean, rinse and cook chana dal according to basic recipe and set aside
2. In a saucepan on medium high, heat canola oil
3. Add cloves sauté for 10 seconds, add diced onions and sauté until golden brown (5-6 minutes)
4. Add tomatoes and sauté for 2 minutes
5. Add mushrooms and sauté for 2 minutes
6. Add coriander, cumin, turmeric, garam masala, red chili and sauté for 30 seconds
7. Add cooked chana dal, salt, reduce heat to medium-low and simmer for 3-4 minutes
8. Add lime juice, top with cilantro and serve in bowls along with roti or rice

. . . .

Note
This dish is typically served with roti or rice.

Garbanzo Bean Curry

Chana Masala

Chana masala is also known as chole masala or chole. It is a flavorful stew made with garbanzo beans cooked in a spicy tomato sauce. Chana masala is typically served with roti, rice, or nan. A bowl of chana masala provides a powerful nutrition punch of protein and fiber.

Ingredients

Makes 4 (6-8 oz each) servings

- 1-28 oz can garbanzo beans, drained and rinsed
- or ~3 cups cooked garbanzo beans
- 1 tablespoon canola oil
- 1.5 teaspoons cumin seeds
- 1 medium-sized onion, chopped
- 1 tablespoon minced garlic
- 1 tablespoon minced ginger
- 1 serrano pepper, minced or finely chopped (optional)
- 1-2 teaspoons garam masala
- 1-1.5 teaspoons coriander
- ½ teaspoon turmeric
- ½-¾ teaspoon salt
- 1 15-oz can diced tomatoes

. . . .

Garnish

- ½-1 cup chopped onions
- ½-1 cup chopped green bell peppers
- ¼ cup chopped cilantro
- Lemon or lime wedges

Method

1. Drain and rinse canned garbanzo beans thoroughly and set aside
2. In a saucepan, heat oil over medium heat and fry cumin seeds until they are fragrant
3. Add onions and sauté until golden brown
4. Lower the heat and add garlic, ginger, serrano chili, garam masala, coriander, turmeric, salt. Stir and cook for ~30 seconds
5. Add tomatoes and cook for a few minutes
6. Raise the heat to medium-high and add garbanzo beans, cook for ~5-10 minutes. If the mixture seems too dry, add some water. When it simmers, turn down the heat, cover and cook for another 5-10 minutes for flavors to come together.
7. Top with garnishes and serve along with rice, roti, puri or whole wheat toast.

Black-Eyed Pea Stew

Chola - *A delicious black-eyed pea stew.*

Black eyed peas also called cowpeas, pack a powerful nutrition punch as a good source of protein and fiber. They also provide potassium, iron, folate and other nutrients. Did you know that when we eat plant-based, iron-rich foods along with vitamin-C rich foods, we can significantly enhance our body's absorption of the iron? Since this recipe includes tomatoes we are naturally enhancing our body's iron absorption from the black-eyed peas.

Ingredients

Serves 4

- 2 cups raw, black eyed peas
- 1 tablespoon oil
- 1 tablespoon cumin seeds
- 1 tablespoon minced garlic
- 1 tablespoon minced ginger
- 1 14-oz can diced tomatoes or 2-3 fresh tomatoes chopped
- 1.5 teaspoons ground coriander
- 1.5 teaspoons ground cumin
- 1.5 teaspoons turmeric
- 1 teaspoon salt
- 2-4 tablespoons finely chopped cilantro

Method

1. Soak black-eyed peas in water overnight or for 4-6 hours, rinse and cook them either in a large pot or in your pressure cooker/Instant pot. Set aside
2. Heat oil on medium high
3. Add cumin seeds and sauté until dark brown
4. Add garlic, ginger, tomato, dry spices and cook for 2-3 minutes
5. Add cooked black-eyed peas, mix well
6. Turn down the heat to low, cover and cook for ~4-5 minutes
7. Add cilantro and serve with rice or roti

Moong Dal with Spinach

Keerai Kootu

A delicious split green lentils and spinach stew. Keerai is the Tamil word for leafy greens. Traditionally, this recipe is served as a side dish with rice or roti. You could also enjoy a bowl of the stew as is for a light dinner with a side salad. The combination of spinach, lentils and spices make it a healthy and iron-rich food choice that is substantial and satisfying.

Ingredients

Serves 4

- 2 cups cooked moong dal
- 1.5 teaspoons oil
- 1 teaspoon cumin seeds
- ½ teaspoon asafetida (optional)
- 1 cup chopped onions
- 1 teaspoon minced ginger
- 1-2 green chili, deseeded and chopped (optional)
- ½ cup chopped tomatoes
- 2 cups water
- 4 cups tightly packed spinach leaves
- 1 teaspoon ground turmeric
- 1 teaspoon ground red chili (optional)
- 1 teaspoon salt
- 1 teaspoon lime or lemon juice (optional)

Method

1. Rinse, clean and cook moong dal (split green lentils) following the basic recipe with your pressure cooker, Instant pot or on the stovetop and set aside
2. Heat oil in a saucepan on medium high, add cumin seeds and asafetida. Sauté for 15-30 seconds until seeds turn a darker brown
3. Add onions and sauté until they turn golden brown ~3-4 minutes
4. Add ginger, green chili, tomatoes and sauté for 1 minute
5. Add cooked moong dal, water, spinach leaves, turmeric, red chili and salt
6. Reduce heat to low and simmer for 5'
7. Turn off the heat, add lemon or lime juice and mix
8. Serve in bowls and enjoy as is or with rice or roti

Red Lentil Soup

Masoor Dal - *Indian name for split red lentils.*

Whole red lentils, when skinned and split, show an orange-colored lentil which, interestingly, turns yellow in color when cooked. Split red lentils are easily available in grocery stores. This dal is usually served with rice or roti (round flatbread). I enjoy serving it as a soup and it is always a favorite when entertaining friends at our home.

Ingredients

Serves 4

- ✿ 2 cups cooked masoor dal (split and skinned red lentils)
- ✿ 1 tablespoon canola oil
- ✿ 1 teaspoon cumin seeds
- ✿ 4-6 whole cloves
- ✿ 1 cup diced onions
- ✿ ½ cup diced fresh or canned tomatoes
- ✿ 1 teaspoon minced garlic
- ✿ 1 teaspoon turmeric
- ✿ ½ teaspoon ground red chili (optional)
- ✿ ¼ cup tomato sauce, canned (optional)
- ✿ 1 teaspoon salt
- ✿ 1 cup water
- ✿ 2 tablespoons finely chopped cilantro

Method

1. Sort, clean, rinse and cook 1 cup masoor dal with 2 cups water according to the basic recipe. You will have 2 cups cooked dal, set aside
2. Heat oil in a saucepan on medium high, add cumin seeds and sauté until fragrant 10-15 seconds
3. Add cloves and sauté for 10 seconds
4. Add onions and sauté until golden brown ~5-6 minutes
5. Add tomatoes, garlic and cook for 2 minutes
6. Add turmeric, red chili, tomato sauce and sauté for 30 seconds
7. Add cooked masoor dal, salt, water, mix well, and reduce heat to medium-low
8. Simmer for 3-4 minutes
9. Add cilantro, turn off the stove and serve into bowls
10. Enjoy as a soup, or with rice or roti

Kidney Beans in a Spicy Sauce

Rajma - *Kidney beans simmered in a delicious onion and tomato sauce*

Rajma is one of my all time favorite dishes and I have to share a story about my connection to it.

My school cafeteria (we called it canteen) in Madras had delicious vegetarian food choices every day for lunch. I typically took a homemade lunch to school every day. One day, I had forgotten my lunch and so bought it at school. I tasted rajma and rice for my first time when in elementary school. It was so tasty and satisfying. I rushed home and told my mom all about it. She was not familiar with rajma as it was not common in Gujarat (where she was from) or Madras (where we lived). Rajma is a popular dish from the Northern Indian state of Punjab. I described the bean, the flavor profile and my mom managed to recreate it at home for us. It became part of our family meal rotations and I continue to enjoy making it for my family. For a classic pairing enjoy Rajma with some plain rice or roti. You can also enjoy it as a comforting bowl of Indianized Vegetarian Chili.

Ingredients

Serves 4

- 1 tablespoon oil
- 1 teaspoon cumin seeds
- 1 cinnamon stick
- 4-6 cloves
- 2-3 bay leaves
- 1.5 cups chopped onion
- 1 28 oz can tomatoes in juice
- 1 teaspoon minced garlic
- 1 teaspoon turmeric
- 1 teaspoon ground cumin
- 1 teaspoon ground coriander
- ¼ teaspoon ground red chili
- 2 29 oz cans, kidney beans
- 1 cup water
- 1 teaspoon garam masala
- 1 teaspoon salt

Method

1. Heat oil in a deep pan on high
2. Add cumin seeds, cinnamon, cloves and bay leaves. Sauté for 2 minutes
3. Turn down heat to medium-high
4. Add chopped onions, sauté until golden brown
5. Add diced tomatoes in juice, minced garlic, spices (excluding garam masala), cook for 2 minutes
6. Turn off heat, blend using a blender/food processor or immersion blender
7. Put blended ingredients back in deep pan o the stove on medium high setting
8. Add drained and rinsed kidney beans, add water, garam masala, salt and bring to a boil
9. Lower heat, cover and simmer on low for 2-3 minutes
10. Turn off the stove and enjoy

Split Pigeon Pea and Vegetables Stew

Sambar - *A mixed vegetable and split pigeon pea stew*

Sambar is a lentil stew made from tuvar dal (split pigeon peas) with a variety of vegetables and traditionally served with rice, dosai (crispy lentil and rice crepe), idly (steamed fermented rice and lentil cake), and other south Indian dishes. Depending upon the choice of vegetable used, the name of the sambar changes. For example, onion sambar, tomato sambar, sambar with okra, etc. Since it is made on a daily basis, highlighting different vegetables changes up the flavor profile and keeps it more interesting. In the recipe below, I am sharing a mixed vegetable sambar. You can substitute or add other fresh or frozen vegetables. Sambar powder is a blend of spices such as coriander, cumin, red chili, turmeric, fenugreek, asafetida) that adds a unique flavor to sambar. I have included my recipe for homemade sambar powder in the basic recipes. You can also find sambar powder online or at Indian grocery stores.

Ingredients
Serves 4-6

- 2 cups cooked (split pigeon peas) tuvar dal
- 1 tablespoon canola oil
- 1 cup diced onions
- 1 cup diced fresh or canned tomatoes
- ½ cup thinly sliced carrots
- 1 cup diced zucchini
- ½ cup water
- 1 tablespoon tamarind paste or concentrate
- 3 tablespoons sambar powder
- 1 teaspoon salt

....

Tempering
- 1 teaspoon ghee or oil
- 1 teaspoon whole, black mustard seeds
- ¼ teaspoon asafetida
- 1 dried red chili broken into 2 pieces (optional)
- 5-6 curry leaves (optional)

Method

1. Sort, clean, rinse and cook split pigeon peas by following basic recipe instructions, puree, and set aside
2. In a saucepan on medium high flame, heat canola oil and add onions
3. Sauté until onions turn golden brown 6-7 minutes
4. Add tomatoes and cook for 2-3 minutes
5. Add carrots and zucchini, water and cook for another 3-5 minutes until all the vegetables are tender
6. Add sambar powder, tamarind paste, and salt
7. Reduce the heat to low and simmer for 2-3 minutes
8. Add pureed dal, mix well and simmer for another 2-3 minutes
9. If the mixture is too thick, add ¼ cup water at a time as needed to dilute to an appropriate consistency. Sambar is typically not too thick or thin
10. Tempering - In a small pan, heat ghee and add whole black mustard seeds. When they pop in 10-15 seconds, add asafetida, red chili pieces, curry leaves and turn off the heat
11. Drizzle the tempering mix into the saucepan, mix well and simmer for another 4-5 minutes to ensure all the flavors are blended and serve with rice or as an accompaniment to idli or dosai

Garbanzo Beans with Coconut and Spices

Chana Sundal or Vellai Kondakadalai Sundal

A coconut spiced garbanzo bean side dish. This is often prepared and served during festivals in south India. Every Sunday, my family had the tradition of going to the Marina beach in Madras. While we sat on the cool sand, we often snacked on freshly roasted corn, green mango topped with chili, or sundal from local vendors. Sundal is the generic term used for a side dish made from a variety of beans prepared with coconut and spices.

Ingredients

Serves 4

- ✿ 2 cups cooked garbanzo beans
- ✿ 1 teaspoon oil
- ✿ 1 teaspoon whole, black mustard seeds or cumin seeds
- ✿ ¼ teaspoon asafetida
- ✿ 1 teaspoon minced ginger
- ✿ 1-2 green chili, deseeded and diced (optional)
- ✿ 1 whole dried red chili broken into 3-4 pieces (optional)
- ✿ ¼ cup shredded unsweetened coconut
- ✿ ½ teaspoon salt (adjust per your taste)
- ✿ 1 teaspoon lime juice
- ✿ 2 tablespoons cilantro, finely chopped

Method

1. Soak and cook garbanzo beans or use a can of garbanzo beans - drain and set aside. If using canned beans, rinse thoroughly at least two to three times to decrease sodium content.
2. Heat oil in a skillet on medium-high and add mustard or cumin seeds
3. As soon as the seeds start to pop, add asafetida, ginger, chili and sauté for 15-30 seconds
4. Add cooked garbanzo beans, coconut, continue to sauté for a few minutes
5. Turn off the stove, add lime juice, cilantro and mix well
6. Enjoy as a delicious side dish or a warm, savory snack

Sprouted Moong Bean Salad

Fangavela Mag - *Sprouted Moong Bean Salad*

This is a crunchy and savory salad that can be enjoyed as a snack or along with rice or roti. Sprouted moong beans are lower in calories compared to moong beans, and provide a higher amount of amino acids and antioxidants. They are a good source of protein, fiber, B vitamins, vitamin C and vitamin K.

Ingredients
Serves 6

. . . .

Dressing
- ☼ 1 tablespoon oil (olive or canola)
- ☼ 1/2 to 1 teaspoon salt (optional)
- ☼ 1 teaspoon ground cumin
- ☼ 1 tablespoon lemon juice

. . . .

Beans
- ☼ 2 cups sprouted moong (also known as mung) beans
- ☼ Salt, to taste
- ☼ 1 cup chopped tomatoes
- ☼ 1 cup chopped cucumber
- ☼ 1/2 to 1 cup shredded cabbage
- ☼ 1 seeded and diced green chili (optional)
- ☼ 1 teaspoon minced ginger (optional)
- ☼ 1/4 cup chopped cilantro

Method
1. Sprout moong beans according to the basic recipe and set aside
2. Mix all of the dressing ingredients and set aside
3. Heat 1/4 cup of water in a pan with sprouts and salt. When it comes to a boil, turn the stove off, and leave it covered for 4 to 5 minutes
4. Mix the sprouted beans with all of the ingredients, stir in the dressing, and top with cilantro

. . . .

Note
Moong bean sprouts can be a source of bacteria. Although you will lose some of the nutrients, cooked sprouts are safer as it will destroy any potential bacteria.

Vibrant Veggies

Vegetables are an important part of a healthy way of eating. This section features colorful vegetables prepared with an array of spices creating unique and flavorful vegetable dishes. You will find coconut and mustard used more commonly in the south Indian style vegetables and garam masala in the north Indian style vegetables.

Oven Roasted, Spiced Cauliflower

Phool Gobi Sabji - *Phool gobi is the Hindi name for cauliflower and sabji is the word to describe vegetables in the raw or cooked form.*

A golden-hued roasted cauliflower dish that comes together very easily and quickly. Cauliflower is a good source of vitamin K, vitamin C, fiber, folate, antioxidants and phytonutrients. You can enjoy this recipe as a side dish, or add it to your salad greens for a warm and beautiful salad course.

Ingredients

Serves 4

- 2 tablespoons canola oil
- 1 teaspoon cumin seeds
- 1 teaspoon turmeric
- 1 teaspoon garam masala
- ½ teaspoon chili powder (optional)
- 1 large head of cauliflower cut into 1" florets (4-6 cups)
- 1 teaspoon salt
- 1 teaspoon lime juice
- ¼ cup finely chopped cilantro

Method

1. Preheat oven to 450 degrees Fahrenheit
2. Line a baking sheet with foil and set aside
3. Add all the ingredients except lime juice and cilantro in a large bowl or plastic bag to toss and evenly coat the florets with spice blend
4. Spread florets in a single layer on lined baking sheet
5. Place in the top or center of oven
6. Roast for 15 minutes until the florets turn brown around the edges and are crisp but tender
7. Transfer to a serving bowl or platter.
8. Add lime juice, mix well, garnish with cilantro and serve with bread or rice

Potato and Onion Mash

Potato Masala

A delicious turmeric and ginger spiced vegetable side dish that has the texture of mashed potatoes. Potatoes provide vitamin C, potassium, some fiber, and trace amounts of B vitamins, magnesium, iron and zinc.

This vegetable side dish is often served with puri (fried bread), roti or even used as a stuffing for a south Indian crepe called dosai, or stuffed in a hot grilled sandwich.

Ingredients

Serves 4

- ✿ 2 washed potatoes
- ✿ 1 tablespoon oil
- ✿ 2 teaspoons mustard seeds
- ✿ 1 tablespoon chana dal
- ✿ ¼ teaspoon asafetida
- ✿ 1 cup chopped onions
- ✿ 1 teaspoon minced ginger
- ✿ 1-2 green chili (deseeded and chopped) - optional
- ✿ 5 curry leaves, fresh or dry (optional)
- ✿ 1 teaspoon salt
- ✿ 1 teaspoon turmeric
- ✿ ½ cup water
- ✿ 1 tablespoon lime juice
- ✿ ¼ cup finely chopped cilantro

Method

1. Microwave washed potatoes according to your microwave instructions. Peel and chop into cubes. Makes about 2 cups. Set aside
2. Heat oil in a pan on medium-high
3. Add mustard seeds, chana dal, asafetida, curry leaves
4. When the seeds start popping, add onions, ginger, chili and fry until onions turn golden brown
5. Add salt, turmeric, water
6. When the water starts boiling, add potatoes
7. Stir well and decrease heat to low
8. When thickened, turn off the stove
9. Add lime juice, stir well
10. Garnish with cilantro and serve

Green Bean and Coconut Stir Fry

Green Beans Poriyal - *A delicious coconut and spice-infused green beans stir-fry*

This style of vegetable side dish is very common in south India. You can vary up the vegetables and use the same method.

Ingredients

Serves 4-6

- 1 tablespoon oil
- ½ teaspoon asafetida
- 1 tablespoon urad dal (optional)
- 2 green chili - deseeded and chopped (optional)
- 4 cups frozen green beans or fresh, stringed green beans cut into 1" pieces
- ⅓-½ cup water
- ¾ teaspoon salt
- ⅓ cup shredded, unsweetened coconut

Method

1. Heat oil in a pan on medium high
2. Add hing, urad dal, green chili and sauté for 1 minute until dal is golden brown
3. Add green beans, water, stir, cover and reduce heat to low.
4. Cook for ~5-6 minutes until green beans are tender and cooked
5. Add coconut, salt, mix well and cook for 2 minutes
6. Turn off the stove and enjoy

Zucchini Tomato Curry

Rasawala zucchini kanda tameta nu shaak - *Zucchini cooked in a delicious onion and tomato sauce makes for a colorful side dish.*

Although India has many amazing vegetables (many that are unavailable in America), I had not tried zucchini until I arrived in Los Angeles. Zucchini is available year around, summer is when it is especially abundant. I was inspired to create this recipe after a visit to our local farmers market. To maximize the nutritional benefits, use zucchini with its peel (of course after you wash and clean it well). Zucchini is low in calories, high in water content and provides vitamins and minerals.

Ingredients

Serves 4
* 1 tablespoon oil
* 1 teaspoon cumin seeds
* ¼ teaspoon asafetida
* 1 onion, chopped
* 1 green chili deseeded and chopped (optional)
* 2 tomatoes, chopped
* 3 cups zucchini, washed and chopped
* 1 teaspoon ginger minced
* 1 teaspoon turmeric
* 1.5 teaspoons ground coriander
* 1.5 teaspoons ground cumin
* 1 teaspoon salt

Method

1. Heat oil in a saucepan on medium high
2. Add cumin seeds and sauté for 1 minute
3. Add onions and cook until golden brown
4. Add tomatoes, green chili, dry spices. Sauté for 1 minute
5. Add zucchini and water. Mix well, cover and reduce heat to low
6. Cook for ~5 minutes until zucchini is tender and cooked
7. Stir, garnish and enjoy with chapati, puri, khichdi or as a stew with some bread

Carrot Stir Fry

Gajar Nu Shaak

A tasty stir fry of carrots and spices. It comes together very quickly and adds a colorful and spicy addition to a meal. Enjoy it as an easy and healthy side dish. Gajar is the Gujarati word for carrots and shak means vegetable or vegetable dish in Gujarati. Carrots are an excellent source of antioxidants especially beta carotene, high in fiber and low in calories.

Ingredients

Makes 4 ½ cup servings
- ❁ 1 teaspoon oil
- ❁ 1 teaspoon cumin seeds
- ❁ ¼ teaspoon asafetida
- ❁ 2 cups sliced baby carrots or diced carrots
- ❁ 1 teaspoon ground coriander
- ❁ 1 teaspoon ground cumin
- ❁ ½ teaspoon ground red chili
- ❁ ½ teaspoon salt

Method

1. Heat oil in a skillet on medium-high
2. Add cumin seeds, asafetida, and sauté until fragrant
3. Add all the other ingredients and stir fry for 3-4 minutes
4. Turn off the stove and enjoy with roti or a rice dish

Spinach with Tofu

Palak Tofu - *My vegan version of the popular dish, Saag Paneer.*

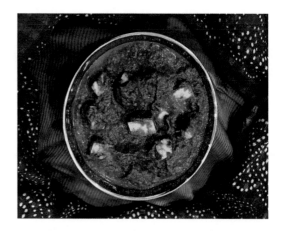

Cubed tofu simmered in a spiced spinach sauce makes for a delicious side dish with rice or bread. Diluted, this might even work as a tasty soup.

Ingredients

Makes 4 servings

- ✿ 1 tablespoon oil
- ✿ 2 whole black cardamoms or 3-4 green cardamom pods
- ✿ 3-4 whole black peppercorns
- ✿ 5 cloves
- ✿ 2 c chopped onions
- ✿ 1.5 tablespoons minced ginger
- ✿ 1.5 tablespoons minced garlic
- ✿ 1-2 green chili - deseeded and chopped (optional)
- ✿ 1 cup chopped tomatoes (fresh or canned)
- ✿ 1 pound spinach (fresh, prepackaged or frozen)
- ✿ ½ - ¾ cup water
- ✿ 1 teaspoon salt
- ✿ 1 teaspoon garam masala
- ✿ ½ teaspoon ground red chili (optional)
- ✿ 1 12-16 ounce package firm tofu, drained and cubed

Method

1. Heat oil in a medium saucepan on medium high heat
2. Add cardamom, peppercorns, cloves and sauté for 30 seconds to release the aroma
3. Add onions, sauté until they turn light brown
4. Add ginger, garlic and sauté for 1 minute
5. Add tomatoes and cook for 1-2 minutes
6. Add spinach, water, salt, garam masala and red chili. Cover and cook for 4 minutes
7. Blend all of the ingredients in a blender or by using an immersion blender
8. Add tofu, cook for another 2-4 minutes
9. On medium-high heat ghee in a small pan until melted, add red chili, sauté for 5- 10 seconds and remove immediately from stove
10. Drizzle the optional topping on palak tofu

• •

Optional topping for those who like it spicy
1 tablespoon ghee, 1 teaspoon ground red chili

Corn Curry

Makkai Nu Shaak - An Indian spiced version of a warm corn salad.

I was inspired to create this recipe on a warm summer day after a big haul of fresh corn from our local farmers market. The spices and coconut are reminiscent of flavors of Sundal which reminds me of carefree Sundays on Madras beach as a child. Corn is a good source of fiber, vitamin C, magnesium, potassium, folate and phytonutrients.

Ingredients

Makes 4 servings

- 1 tablespoon oil
- 1 teaspoon cumin seeds
- 1 cup chopped onions
- 1 green chili, deseeded and chopped (optional)
- 1 teaspoon minced ginger
- 4 cups frozen corn or fresh off the cob
- 1 teaspoon salt
- 1 cup water
- ¼ cup shredded, unsweetened coconut
- ¼ cup finely chopped cilantro

Method

1. Heat oil in a medium saucepan on medium high heat
2. Add cumin seeds and sauté for 1 minute (ensure that the cumin seeds do not turn black or burn)
3. Add onions, green chili, ginger and sauté for ~3 minutes until onions turn a golden brown
4. Add corn, water, salt, cover and cook until all the water is absorbed (5-7 minutes)
5. Add coconut and cook for 1 minute
6. Turn off the stove, garnish with cilantro and enjoy as a side dish with roti

Eggplant and Pea Curry

Ringna Vatana Nu Shaak - *My lightened version of an eggplant and green peas stir-fry dish popular in Gujarat*

Eggplants are a nutrient dense food and provide a variety of nutrients for a low calorie impact. They are a good source of fiber, antioxidants, polyphenols and more. They provide many positive health benefits including reduce our risk for heart disease, help with blood sugar control, and weight management.

Enjoy this flavorful recipe with roti, a rice dish or khichdi. This also makes a unique side dish to enjoy with a protein and grain of your choice.

Ingredients

Makes 4 servings

- 1 tablespoon oil
- 1 tablespoon finely chopped ginger
- 1-2 green chili- deseeded and chopped (optional)
- 1 teaspoon garlic
- 1 tablespoon ground coriander
- 1 tablespoon ground cumin
- 1.5 teaspoon ground red chili (optional)
- 2 cups eggplant cut into 1" pieces
- 1 cup water
- 1 teaspoon salt
- 1 cup chopped tomatoes (fresh or canned)
- 1 cup frozen green peas
- 2-3 tablespoons finely chopped cilantro

Method

1. Heat oil in a pan on medium high
2. Add ginger, chili, garlic and dry spices. Sauté for ~30 seconds
3. Add eggplant, mix well and reduce heat to low
4. Add water, cover and cook for 4 minutes
5. Add green peas, tomatoes, mix well, cover and cook ~2-4 minutes until peas and eggplant are tender
6. Taste and adjust salt per your preference
7. Garnish with cilantro and serve

Daikon with Green Tops and Garbanzo Bean Flour Curry

Mooli nu shaak - *A unique vegetable side dish that incorporates garbanzo bean flour with daikon and daikon greens.*

Ingredients
Makes 4 servings
- ✿ 1 teaspoon oil
- ✿ 2 cups peeled and chopped daikon 1" cubes
- ✿ 2 cups finely chopped daikon greens˙
- ✿ ¼-½ cups water as needed during final cooking steps

....

Garbanzo Bean Flour Mix:
- ✿ ½ cup garbanzo bean flour
- ✿ 1 teaspoon turmeric
- ✿ ¼-½ teaspoon red chili
- ✿ ½ teaspoon ground coriander
- ✿ ½ teaspoon ground cumin
- ✿ 1.5 teaspoons oil
- ✿ ½ teaspoon salt

Method
1. In a small bowl, mix all the Garbanzo Bean Flour Mix ingredients and set aside
2. Heat 1 teaspoon oil in a pan on medium-high heat
3. Add daikon pieces, cover and cook for 2 minutes
4. Add daikon greens, stir, cover and cook for 2 minutes
5. Add Garbanzo Bean Flour Mix, stir, lower heat to low, cover and cook for 2 minutes
6. Add ¼-½ cup water if it looks too dry. Mix well and cook for 1 minute
7. Turn off the stove and enjoy with roti or puri

....

Note
Using all edible parts of fruits and vegetables is a common practice in India to minimize food wastage. When I first visited farmers markets near my home in Los Angeles, I remember seeing huge daikons stacked in beautiful rows but the green tops were all removed and discarded. When I would ask the vendors if I could pay for the greens - they would ask me if the greens were for my pet. Interestingly, if you buy daikon at an Indian grocery store, you will most likely find it with the green tops intact. Daikon radishes are very low in calories and a good source of vitamin C.

Glorious Grains

A wide variety of grains are used in Indian cuisine. Wheat is the predominant grain in the north and rice is the predominant grain in the south. Other grains such as millets, buckwheat, sorghum are also regularly used. Feel free to substitute brown rice for the white rice used in recipes and note that all the wheat flour used in the recipes are made from whole grain, whole wheat. You may be able to use a gluten free flour substitute for the wheat flour but the recipes may need some adjustments.

....

White Rice

Ingredients

Serves 4

- ⚙ 1 cup uncooked white rice (basmati or long-grained)
- ⚙ 1.5-2 cups water

Method

1. Place rice in a small bowl. Rinse the rice with water while rubbing the grains with your fingers. Drain into a sieve and repeat this process another two or three times.
2. Add drained rice and water into a medium-sized saucepan on high heat. Bring to a boil.
3. Stir, reduce the heat to low and cover the saucepan.
4. Simmer until all the water has been absorbed and you may see tiny shallow holes on the surface indicating water has been absorbed. This takes about 8-10 minutes.
5. Turn off the heat and let the covered saucepan rest for 5 more minutes on the stove.
6. Fluff the rice gently with a fork before serving.

. . . .

Note

It is important to thoroughly wash rice before cooking to ensure it's clean and to remove the starchy residue. Thoroughly rinsed rice will allow for a less sticky grain. This basic rice recipe is used almost daily in South India. This is the rice I use for most of the rice dishes in the book.

Lemon Rice

Elumichai Sadam

This is a refreshing rice dish flavored with fresh lime juice and is commonly prepared in South India. Interestingly, the term lime and lemon are used interchangeably in India even though, it is common to only find limes there. Elumichai is the Tamil name for lemon and sadam is the name for rice. Lemon rice is often served as a religious offering in south Indian temples. It can be enjoyed as is with some potato chips or as a side dish along with a bean/lentil or vegetable dish. I have fond memories of lemon rice being served at my school cafeteria because it was light and flavorful.

Ingredients

Makes 4 (½ cup) servings

- 2 cups cooked plain rice
- 1 tablespoon canola oil
- 1 teaspoon cumin seeds
- 1 teaspoon minced ginger
- 2-3 whole, dried red chili broken in half (optional)
- 1 tablespoon chana dal (yellow split brown garbanzo beans)
- ½ tablespoon urad dal (split, dehusked black lentils) - optional
- ¼ teaspoon asafetida
- 1 green chili, deseeded and cut into strips (optional)
- 1 teaspoon turmeric
- 1 teaspoon salt
- Juice of one lime
- 2 tablespoons finely chopped cilantro
- 2-4 tablespoons roasted peanuts or roasted cashews (optional)

Method

1. Prepare and set aside 2 cups of plain white rice
2. Heat 1 tablespoon oil in a skillet and add cumin, ginger, chana dal, urad dal and asafetida
3. Sauté until cumin is darker brown and lentils are light brown
4. Add green chili or red chili and sauté for a few seconds
5. Add cooked rice, turmeric, salt and mix to combine and heat through
6. Turn off the stove
7. Add juice of lime, mix well
8. Garnish with chopped cilantro and nuts
9. Enjoy immediately while hot or it can be served at room temperature

. . . .

To roast nuts

Heat ½ teaspoon oil in a small pan or wok, add peanuts or cashews and sauté on medium-high heat for 1-2 minutes until golden brown and fragrant. Drain on a paper towel and set aside.

Coconut Rice

Thengai Sadam

This is an aromatic rice dish flavored with coconut and is commonly prepared in south India. Coconuts play an important role in religious ceremonies as well as in Indian cuisine. Thengai is the Tamil name for coconut and sadam is the Tamil name for rice. Coconut rice is often served as a religious offering in south Indian temples. It can be enjoyed as is with some potato chips or as a side dish along with a legume or vegetable dish. You can also pair it with any protein choice and a salad.

Ingredients

Makes 4 (½ cup) servings

- 2 cups cooked plain rice
- 1 teaspoon canola oil
- 2 tablespoons chana dal (yellow split brown garbanzo beans)
- 1 tablespoon urad dal (split, dehusked black lentils) - optional
- ¼ teaspoon asafetida
- 4 whole, dried red chili broken in half (optional)
- 1 cup shredded, unsweetened coconut
- 1 teaspoon salt
- 2-4 tablespoons roasted cashews (optional)

Method

1. Prepare and set aside 2 cups of plain white rice (basic recipe) or use frozen pre-cooked rice
2. Heat oil in a skillet and add chana dal, urad dal and asafetida
3. Sauté until lentils are light brown
4. Add red chili and sauté for a few seconds
5. Add cooked rice, coconut, salt and mix to combine and heat through
6. Turn off the stove
7. Garnish with roasted nuts
8. Enjoy immediately while hot or it can be served at room temperature

....

Roasting cashews

Heat ½ teaspoon oil in a small pan or wok, add cashews and sauté on medium-high heat for 1-2 minutes until golden brown and fragrant. Drain on a paper towel and set aside.

Pulav

Brown Rice Pulav

A fragrant and lightly spiced rice dish seasoned with aromatics. Pulav pairs well with any of the vegetable or legume dishes featured in this book. It can also be enjoyed on its own with cucumber raita for a light meal.

Ingredients

Serves 4
- 1 teaspoon canola oil
- 1 teaspoon cumin seeds
- 1 1-inch cinnamon stick
- 5 cloves
- 4 cardamom
- 2 bay leaves
- ¾ teaspoon salt
- 1 ¾ cup water
- 1 cup quick-cook brown basmati rice

....

Notes

If you like softer rice, add more water when cooking.

To reduce cooking time, consider soaking cleaned and rinsed basmati rice in water for at least 15-30 minutes

Substitute white basmati rice for the quick-cook brown basmati rice

Discard whole spices (cinnamon, cloves, cardamom) when eating

Add 2-4 tablespoons roasted cashews as a garnish for added crunch and flavor

Method

1. Sort, clean and rinse basmati rice a few times and set aside
2. In a saucepan, heat oil and fry whole spices (cumin seeds, cinnamon stick, cloves, cardamom and bay leaf) for ~30 seconds on medium high
3. Slowly add water, rice, salt and bring to a boil
4. Reduce heat to medium-low, cover and simmer for ~10-12 minutes or until the water has been absorbed.
5. Fluff and serve

Peas Pulav

A tasty rice dish made with fragrant spices and vibrant green peas. This quick recipe can upgrade your basic rice into an exciting option. Green peas are a good source of nutrients including fiber and antioxidants.

Ingredients

Serves 4-6

- 1 cup basmati rice
- 1 cup frozen peas
- 1 tablespoon canola oil
- 1 teaspoon cumin seeds
- 2 1-inch cinnamon sticks
- 6 whole cloves
- 5 whole green cardamoms
- 2 bay leaves
- 1-2 green chili deseeded and cut lengthwise into strips (optional)
- ¼ teaspoon ground turmeric
- ½ teaspoon garam masala (optional)
- 2 cups water
- ¾ teaspoon salt (optional)
- ¼ cup finely chopped cilantro

. . . .

Variations

Add 1 cup chopped onions to step 3 and cook until they turn golden brown before moving to step 4

Add 2 teaspoon minced garlic and or minced ginger to step 3

Add 8-10 roasted cashews to the final garnish along with cilantro

Substitute finely chopped mint for cilantro

Method

1. Clean, wash and rinse basmati rice and set aside
2. In a small bowl, place frozen peas and cover them with water to defrost and set aside
3. Heat oil in a saucepan on medium-high, add cumin seeds, cinnamon, cloves, cardamom, bay leaves and sauté until fragrant and cumin turns a darker brown ~10-20 seconds
4. Add green chili and sauté for 10 seconds
5. Add turmeric, garam masala and sauté for 10 seconds
6. Add water and salt bring to a boil
7. Add rice, peas, stir well and bring to a boil
8. Reduce heat to low, cover and cook for 10-15 minutes until rice is done
9. Turn off the stove, add cilantro.
10. Fluff the rice and serve with raita, bean dish or enjoy as a side dish

Indian Flatbread

Roti - Whole Wheat Flatbread

Roti is also known as rotli, fulka, or chapati. It is a flatbread made from whole wheat flour. It may seem complicated, but it can be a lot of fun and nothing tastes as good as a fresh roti. My mom insisted on making fresh roti for each of us as we sat down to eat. Another fond memory surrounding roti is when we were young, my mom would finish up our meal by serving a fresh roti spread with ghee and filled with a light sprinkling of jaggery (called gol in Gujarat) as a sweet treat. Jaggery is made from raw, concentrated sugarcane juice that is boiled and solidified into blocks. Jaggery is thought to have many health benefits and is part of traditional Indian cuisine. You could use sugar in place of jaggery if you wanted to try this sweet treat idea.

Ingredients

Makes 6 rotis
* 1 cup whole wheat flour
* 1 tablespoon canola oil divided into two
* ¼ cup water

....

Tip

I often make a double batch of roti dough and place half in the freezer to be used at a future time. Frozen dough will stay good in the freezer for two to three months. When ready to use, simply thaw and follow the rest of the steps for fresh roti. The same dough with a few additions such as chopped herbs (green onions, cilantro) or spices (cumin, garlic, turmeric) makes a variety of other flatbread options with different Indian names.

Method

1. Place whole wheat flour in a medium-large bowl
2. Create a well in the middle of the flour and add 2 teaspoons oil
3. Use your fingers to mix the oil and flour together until it becomes crumbly
4. Add water a little at a time and mix well until all the flour is mixed together to form a dough
5. Spread 1 teaspoon oil on the palm of your hands, and massage the dough gently, cover the surface with oil
6. Cover and set aside the dough for at least a few minutes
7. Divide the dough into 6 pieces
8. Roll each piece into a ball and gently flatten it with your hands
9. Start heating a nonstick skillet/tava on the stove on medium-high heat
10. Dip each ball in the extra flour before placing on a flat rolling surface
11. Use a rolling pin and gently roll out into a circle as evenly as possible
12. Pick up the rolled out roti with your hands and gently slide it onto the warmed skillet
13. Wait until it is slightly cooked and using tongs flip it over

14. Once you see light brown spots on the bottom, using tongs pick up the roti
15. Remove the skillet and place the roti directly on the flame or electric range, it should start puffing up
16. Turn it over and cook directly over the flame/electric range for a few seconds
17. Set it aside
18. Repeat the same steps for each of the remaining balls
19. Spread ghee or oil if you would like on each roti before serving it
20. Roti is typically enjoyed with any vegetable or legume dishes

Puffed, Fried Bread

Puri

A delicious crispy fried whole wheat bread. Since it is deep fried, puri was prepared and served occasionally at my childhood home. It was often reserved for a special holiday or meal. Puris work well for when you are entertaining because you can make them ahead of time and they taste great even at room temperature. I have fond memories of my mom packing puri and masala potatoes for my school field trip lunches.

Ingredients

Makes 12 puris

- 1 cup whole wheat flour
- 1 tablespoon canola oil
- ⅔-¾ cup water (room temperature)
- ¼ cup whole wheat flour for dusting
- 2-4 cups canola oil for frying

Method

1. Place whole wheat flour in a large bowl
2. Make a well in the center of the flour and add oil
3. Mix with your fingers to a crumbly texture
4. Slowly add water a little at a time to help make a smooth dough
5. Divide dough into 12 pieces and roll into balls
6. Dip each ball in the extra flour for dusting, and roll on a smooth rolling surface into a circle ~3 inches
7. Heat oil in a deep pan
8. Place each circle (puri) in hot oil gently. Press gently with a slotted spoon to help guide the puri to puff up. Turn it over and fry until it is light beige
9. Remove puri with a slotted spoon onto a paper towel lined plate to drain
10. Repeat the same steps for all the puris
11. Enjoy puri with a vegetable or bean/legume dish

Tasty Accompaniments

No Indian meal is complete without flavorful accompaniments. These can range from a chopped salad to sweet or spicy sauces. A small serving of any of these accompaniments can significantly amp up the flavor of your meal. Be creative and use these as dips, spreads or a topping.

Recipes

Cilantro Mint Chutney

Green Chutney

This is a vibrant chutney made with cilantro, mint, green chili, lime, and salt. Green chutney as it is commonly known in India, is served as a dip for Indian appetizers such as samosa, pakoras, dhoklas, or used as a spread in sandwiches and wraps.

Ingredients

Makes 6- 8 (tablespoons) servings

- ☼ 1 cup cilantro leaves
- ☼ ½ cup mint leaves
- ☼ 1-2 green chili (optional - adjust per your spice preference)
- ☼ 1 teaspoon lime juice
- ☼ ½ teaspoon salt
- ☼ 2-4 tablespoons water as needed during the blending process

Method

1. Wash, clean and prep cilantro, mint, green chili, and lime juice
2. Place cilantro, mint, green chili, lime juice, and salt in a blender and crush
3. Add water as needed to form a smooth paste (1 tablespoon at a time)
4. Taste and adjust salt and spice level according to your preference
5. If using as a spread, add less water in the blending process and keep the consistency thicker
6. Store chutney in the refrigerator until ready for use

. . . .

Notes

Use less water if making chutney as a spread and use more water if planning to use it as an accompaniment/dip.

Variations: Add either any one or all of these - 1" piece of ginger, 1-2 garlic cloves, and ½ cup chopped onion in step 2.

Make a bigger batch and freeze some in smaller containers for future use. Simply defrost and have chutney ready to go.

Date Chutney

Khajur Imli chutney

An interesting blend of sweet and tangy flavors make this chutney special. It is a key accompaniment to North Indian dishes such as papdi chaat, bhelpuri, samosa. Dates and tamarind come together in this tasty chutney. Consider using this as a unique spread on your toast or in your wraps. Dates are high in nutrients including fiber and antioxidants. They also provide a delicious natural sweetness. Tamarind is a good source of vitamins and minerals including vitamins B, C, magnesium, phosphorus and fiber.

Ingredients

Makes 1 Cup

- ⚙ 1 cup seedless dates
- ⚙ 1- 2 tablespoons tamarind concentrate/paste
- ⚙ ¼ cup brown sugar
- ⚙ ¼ - ½ teaspoon ground red chili
- ⚙ ½ teaspoon ground cumin
- ⚙ ¼-½ teaspoon salt
- ⚙ 1.5 cups water

Method

1. In a saucepan on medium heat add all the ingredients and simmer for 15-20 minutes
2. Cool slightly and blend with an immersion blender or in a regular blender until smooth
3. Take out into a jar and store for in the refrigerator
4. Serve cool as a delicious dip

Note

Adjust the tangy flavor by reducing the added brown sugar and amount of tamarind concentrate

You can completely eliminate the brown sugar if you choose

Substitute 2-4 tablespoons dried cranberries for the tamarind concentrate in step 1

Adjust water to bring the chutney to the consistency you would like

Coconut Chutney

Thengai Chutney

A fragrant coconut and chili chutney usually served as an accompaniment for south Indian dishes such as dosai, idli, pongal, vadai. Thengai is the Tamil word for coconut. I remember planting a few coconut trees when I was a young child in my parent's home. By the time I was a teenager, we had fully grown coconut trees bearing coconuts in our yard. Our gardener would climb the trees to bring down coconuts that would then be cracked - coconut water would be drunk as a cooling beverage and coconut flesh would be shredded and put to use in various recipes including coconut chutney, coconut rice and coconut ladoo.

Ingredients

Serves 4
- ½ cup shredded, unsweetened coconut
- 2 green chili, deseeded and chopped (optional)
- 2 tablespoons roasted chana dal or raw cashew pieces
- ¼ teaspoon salt
- 4-6 tablespoons water

. . . .

Tempering
- This is an important part of the Indian cooking process. Tempering is the process of heating oil and adding whole or ground spices in rapid succession for a few seconds. The hot oil absorbs the aroma, flavor of the whole spices and this aromatic mixture is then poured over a dish as a finishing touch.
- 1 teaspoon canola oil
- ¼ teaspoon mustard seeds
- 1 teaspoon split, dehusked black lentils (urad dal)
- 4-6 curry leaves (optional)
- ¼ teaspoon asafetida

Method
1. In a blender, crush coconut, green chili, roasted chana dal or cashew pieces, salt and water
2. Take out into a serving bowl
3. Heat oil in a small skillet, add mustard seeds, black lentils, curry leaves and asafetida
4. Sauté until seeds start to pop, turn off the stove
5. Pour the tempering onto the chutney and mix well

Enjoy as a delicious dip with dosai right away or store it in the refrigerator for future use.

. . . .

Variations
Add 1 cup chopped onions to step 3 and cook until they turn golden brown before moving to step 4
Add 2 teaspoons minced garlic and or minced ginger to step 3
Add 8-10 roasted cashews to the final garnish along with cilantro
Substitute finely chopped mint for cilantro

Garlic Chutney

Lasun chutney

A fiery explosion of garlic and chili come together to make this chutney special. It can be added as a spicy addition to any dish you are serving. Think of this as a secret garlic hot sauce that you can pull out anytime to add oomph to your bland dishes. Once prepared, this chutney can be stored and used for up to two weeks. Ensure that it is in an airtight container as it has a strong pungent aroma.

Ingredients

Makes 1 cup

- 25 garlic cloves
- 1 tablespoon ground red chili
- 1 tablespoon lemon juice
- 1 teaspoon ground cumin
- 2 teaspoon ground coriander
- ½ teaspoon salt
- 4-6 tablespoons water

Method

1. Place all the ingredients in a blender and blend into a smooth paste
2. Taste and adjust salt and seasonings according to your preference
3. Add more water if you like it as a thinner sauce

Enjoy this chutney with pudla, rava dosai, drizzled on papdi chaat or wherever you would like an extra spicy and garlicky addition.

Notes

You can use store-bought peeled garlic cloves instead of fresh garlic cloves that you have to peel. You can also use store-bought, minced garlic in place of garlic cloves. Use the conversion on the jar of your minced garlic for the recipe. Generally, ½ teaspoon minced garlic is equal to 1 clove. So, for this recipe you would need ~12.5 teaspoons minced garlic.

Cucumber and Yogurt Dip

Cucumber Raita

A cooling, yogurt and cucumber dip that makes a perfect accompaniment to any spicy dish. Cucumbers are low in calorie and have a high water content. Yogurt provides a good source of protein, calcium, and potassium.

Ingredients

Serves 4

- ✿ 1 cup yogurt
- ✿ ½ cup water
- ✿ 1 cup cucumber (diced or grated)
- ✿ 2-3 tablespoons cilantro, finely chopped
- ✿ ½-1 small serrano chili, minced (optional)
- ✿ Salt (optional)

Method

1. In a bowl, stir the yogurt and water to a smooth consistency
2. Add cucumber, cilantro, chili and salt
3. Mix well, cover and chill before serving

Variations

Substitute finely chopped mint for cilantro

Add 1 teaspoon ground cumin in step 2

Substitute a plant-based yogurt alternative to make this a vegan option

Tomato, Onion, and Cucumber Salad

Kachumber

A quick and easy chopped salad that is often an accompaniment to Indian meals. There are no set rules about vegetables that go into making kachumber. Typically, it includes cucumber, tomato, onion, cilantro, lime/lemon and spices. Enjoy it as a topping to toast, serve it as part of an appetizer platter with crackers or chips, or as a side salad.

Ingredients

Serves 4

- 1.5 cups chopped cucumbers
- 1 cup chopped tomatoes
- ½ cup chopped onions
- ¼ cup chopped cilantro
- 1.5-2 teaspoons freshly squeezed lime or lemon juice
- ¼-½ teaspoon salt
- ½ teaspoon ground cumin
- ¼ teaspoon ground red chili (optional)

Method

1. Wash and prep cucumbers, tomatoes, onions, cilantro
2. In a bowl, combine all the ingredients, mix well and adjust spice level and salt according to your taste preference
3. Serve immediately or store in the refrigerator to cool until you are ready to enjoy

. . . .

Note

You can substitute green onions for regular onions in this recipe
You could also skip onions completely
Substitute finely chopped mint leaves for cilantro

Flavorful Light Meals

This is one of my favorite sections of the book and I hope you enjoy these recipes as well. Typically, some of these are served as breakfast or tea time snacks (called Tiffin in south India). However, I find that these can make a perfect light meal especially on a weeknight.

Savory Cream of Wheat and Vegetable Porridge

Vegetable Upma

A savory veggie-loaded, cream of wheat dish. Traditionally, this is prepared with semolina (called rava in India). However, I prefer to use cream of wheat as it's higher in iron, calcium, and easily available in your local store. You can use regular (2.5 minute or 1 minute) cream of wheat. Upma can be made simply with a few spices and seasonings but I like to load it up with veggies to enhance the nutritional profile as well as flavor.

Ingredients
Serves 4
- ✿ 1 tablespoon canola oil
- ✿ 1 teaspoon cumin seeds
- ✿ ¼ teaspoon asafetida
- ✿ 1 cup finely chopped onions
- ✿ 4-6 curry leaves (optional)
- ✿ 1 green chili, de-seeded and cut into 4 (optional)
- ✿ 1 cup grated or finely chopped carrots
- ✿ 1 cup green peas (optional)
- ✿ 1 tablespoon minced ginger
- ✿ 4 cups water
- ✿ 1 teaspoon salt
- ✿ 1 cup cream of wheat
- ✿ 1 lime (juiced)
- ✿ ¼ cup finely chopped cilantro
- ✿ 1 teaspoon ghee or coconut oil (optional)

Method
1. Heat oil in a wok/pan on medium-high setting
2. Add cumin seeds, asafetida
3. Add onion, curry leaves and sauté until onion turns golden brown
4. Add green chili, carrots, peas, ginger - sauté for 1-2 minutes
5. Add 4 cups of water, salt, and bring to a boil
6. Turn down heat, slowly add cream of wheat while stirring continuously to minimize any lumps
7. Cover and cook for 2 minutes, turn off the stove
8. Add lime juice, ghee or coconut oil mix well and top with cilantro

Enjoy as is or with a coconut or green chutney on the side

....

Variations
Add chopped green onions instead of cilantro in step 8

Add chopped and roasted cashews or peanuts for adding crunch and nutrition in step 8

Garbanzo Flour Crepes

Pudla - Bean-based Crepes

A tasty, gluten-free crepe made from garbanzo bean flour that can be enjoyed as is, stuffed with a filling or made into a vegan omelette.

Ingredients

Serves 4-6

Makes 10-12 pudlas or 6-8 vegan omelettes

- 1 cup Garbanzo bean flour (besan)
- ½ cup water
- 1 teaspoon red chili powder
- ½ teaspoon turmeric
- 1 tablespoon cumin seeds
- 1 tablespoon minced garlic
- ¾ teaspoon salt
- 4 oz firm tofu
- 2 cups finely chopped spinach
- 1 cup finely chopped onion
- 2-3 tablespoons oil

. . . .

To make a veggie omelette

Use the same batter but instead of spreading it out very thin, keep it to the size of a pancake

Add chopped onions, tomatoes, bell peppers, mushrooms and cook a little longer since it will be thicker

Method

1. Mix Garbanzo bean flour, water, spices, garlic, tofu and salt in a blender or by hand in a bowl to a crepe consistency batter. Add more water if needed.
2. Add finely chopped spinach and chopped onions
3. Heat a pan on medium-high, spray with a cooking spray or cover with a tsp of oil
4. Add a ladle of batter (¼ cup) and slowly spread outwards in a circular movement until you have a large circle
5. Add a few drops of oil around the periphery of the crepe and when it looks like the bottom is a darker brown, flip and cook for a few minutes on the other side
6. Enjoy as is or with some green chutney

Lightly Spiced Rice and Lentil Dish

Khichdi

A traditional rice and lentil dish that is comforting and delicious. Khichdi is often served as one of the first foods to a baby. Since it is soft and easy to digest, it is also a good choice when you are feeling sick. I think of khichdi as a warm hug in a bowl.

Ingredients
Makes 4-6 servings
- ⚙ 1 tablespoon canola oil
- ⚙ 1 teaspoon cumin seeds
- ⚙ 10 whole black peppercorns
- ⚙ 2 1-inch cinnamon sticks
- ⚙ 5 whole cloves
- ⚙ ½ teaspoon ground turmeric
- ⚙ 4-5 cups water
- ⚙ ¾ teaspoon salt
- ⚙ 1 cup moong dal (split and hulled green lentils)
- ⚙ 1 cup basmati or any long grain rice
- ⚙ 1 tablespoon ghee or oil
- ⚙ ½ cup water (optional) for final mixing stage if you like it mushier

....

A few variations to khichdi
-Add ½ - 1 teaspoon minced garlic or ginger in step 2
- Add 1 cup diced onions in step 2
- Add 1-1.5 cup diced mixed vegetables fresh or frozen in step 3
- Use quinoa instead of rice in the recipe above
- Use red lentils (masoor) instead of moong dal (split and hulled green lentils)

Method
1. Heat oil in a saucepan over medium high
2. Add cumin seeds, peppercorns, cinnamon sticks and clove - sauté for 30 seconds
3. Add turmeric, water and salt to the saucepan and bring to a boil
4. Clean, sort and wash rice and lentils 2-3 times. Drain and add to the boiling water.
5. Mix and bring to a boil again
6. Cover with a lid partially and cook until almost all the water is absorbed ~10 minutes
7. Reduce heat to low, cover the saucepan completely and cook until rice and lentils are done ~15-20 minutes
8. Add 1 tablespoon ghee or oil and mix thoroughly with a wooden spoon to a slightly mushy consistency
9. Add more water if you like it with a smoother and thinner consistency
10. Turn off the stove, and enjoy khichdi as is or with a vegetable dish, salad, or plain yogurt

....

Notas
Discard whole spices (black peppercorns, cinnamon sticks, cloves) when eating unless you like the extra punch of spice

Cream of Wheat Crepes

Rava Dosai

A semolina based crispy crepe. The most common dosai (crispy crepe) is made from a fermented batter of rice and lentils. However, that is a longer process as it requires soaking the rice and lentils overnight, crushing it and then allowing it to ferment to create a sourdough. Rava dosai is an almost instant version made from semolina and rice flour. I have used cream of wheat instead of semolina as it is more readily available and more nutritious.

Ingredients

Makes 8-10 dosai

- 1 cup cream of wheat (2.5 or 1 minute)
- ½ cup rice flour
- ½ cup finely chopped onions
- 1 teaspoon cumin seeds
- 1 green chili deseeded and finely chopped
- ¾ teaspoon salt
- 1-2 cups water
- 2-3 tablespoons oil

....

Note

When making dosai, it is important to mix the batter each time with a ladle before you pour it on the skillet since the flour may settle in the bottom

Method

1. Add cream of wheat, rice flour, onions, cumin, chili, salt and water into a blender
2. Blend for a few seconds to mix all the ingredients and eliminate any pieces
3. Pour into a bowl and set aside for at least 15 minutes
4. Using a ladle mix the batter and adjust water and salt as needed. The batter needs to be thinner than pancake batter
5. Heat a non-stick skillet on medium-high
6. Spray with cooking spray
7. Take one ladle of batter ~¼ cup and pour onto the heated skillet in a circle
8. Fill any gaps with batter
9. Add a few drops of oil around the edges and cook for 1-2 minutes
10. When the edges look crispy, use a spatula and gently lift and flip over
11. Cook for a minute and remove dosai
12. Repeat until you have used up all the batter
13. Serve hot rava dosai with chutney and sambar

Steamed Garbanzo Flour Cakes

Khaman Dhokla

Khaman dhokla is a steamed, soft and spongy, savory cake. It is made from garbanzo bean flour and is a specialty of Gujarat. Traditionally, it is served as a snack, appetizer or as part of a meal.

Ingredients

Makes 2-4 servings

- 1 cup garbanzo bean flour
- 1 tablespoon cream of wheat
- 1 teaspoon lemon/lime juice
- ½ teaspoon salt
- 1.5 teaspoons sugar
- 1 teaspoon minced ginger
- ½ teaspoon minced green chili (optional)
- ¾-1 cup water
- 1 teaspoon canola oil divided into 2 (½ for batter and ½ for coating 9" inch round pan)
- 1.5 teaspoons Eno - fruit salt

....

Tempering

- 2 teaspoons canola oil
- 1.5 teaspoons cumin seeds
- 2-4 green chilies, deseeded and cut into strips (optional)
- ¼ teaspoon asafetida (optional)

....

Garnish

- 1-2 tablespoons finely chopped cilantro

Method

1. Grease a 9" non-stick round cake pan or dhokla thali (available in Indian stores) with ½ tsp oil or with a cooking spray and set aside
2. Set up a steamer with adequate water to steam and one that can hold the 9" pan
3. In a bowl, mix garbanzo bean flour, cream of wheat, lime juice, salt, sugar, ginger, green chili, water, oil
4. Using your hands mix the batter well to introduce more air ~30-45 seconds
5. Add Eno and mix well to incorporate more air ~30 seconds - the batter should almost double in size and feel fluffy
6. Pour the batter immediately into the prepared round pan
7. Place the pan in the steamer, cover and steam for 10-12 minutes on a medium flame
8. Test with a toothpick, when toothpick comes out clean, remove pan from steamer and set aside to cool a few minutes
9. Using a knife, cut into long pieces, turn the pan around and cut again at a diagonal to create diamond/square shaped pieces
10. In a small pan, heat oil on medium-high
11. Add cumin seeds, green chilies and asafetida - fry for 20-30 seconds until seeds turn a darker brown
12. Pour the tempering onto cut dhokla pieces and place pieces in a serving platter/bowl or individual bowls
13. Garnish with cilantro and enjoy with green chutney

Note

The key to soft dhokla is the batter mixing process (incorporating air) and adding Eno to appropriately ferment the batter. It is very important to place the batter after adding Eno immediately into the steamer to maximize the benefit and create soft dhoklas. Eno fruit salt is available in Indian grocery stores. If Eno is not available, you can substitute with 1 teaspoon baking powder. To make this dish gluten free, you can skip the cream of wheat.

Variations

In the tempering, add ½ teaspoon mustard seeds, ½ teaspoon sesame seeds along with cumin seeds.

For the garnish, you can add any one or all of these especially if enjoying as a light meal - 2 tablespoons finely chopped green onions, 2 tablespoons shredded, unsweetened coconut, 2-4 tablespoons pomegranate arils, ½ cup chopped tomatoes, ½ cup chopped cucumber, ¼-½ cup roasted peanuts or cashews

Scrambled Tofu and Veggies

Tofu Bhurji

A Spicy Veggie and Tofu Scramble. Tofu is an excellent source of plant protein and provides a variety of vitamins and minerals. It may help decrease our risk for heart disease, diabetes, and some types of cancer. Since tofu is like a blank canvas, it takes on the flavors of anything added to it. This recipe with the wide variety of vegetables and spices turns tofu into a delicious choice.

Ingredients

Serves 4

- 1 16 oz package, firm tofu
- 1 tablespoon oil
- 1 teaspoon cumin seeds
- 1 cup onions cut into small pieces
- 1 cup bell pepper cut into small pieces
- 1 cup mushrooms, cut into small pieces
- 4 cups spinach leaves cut into strips or 1 small bag frozen, cut, spinach leaves
- ¾ teaspoon turmeric
- ½ teaspoon ground red chili (optional)
- ½ teaspoon garam masala
- ½ teaspoon salt
- 1-2 tablespoons finely chopped cilantro

Method

1. Drain tofu, pat with paper towels and set aside with a weight on top to drain any more liquid
2. Heat oil in a saucepan, add cumin seeds
3. Add onions and sauté for 2 minutes
4. Add bell peppers, mushrooms, spinach and sauté for 2-3 minutes
5. Crumble tofu and add to the pan along with turmeric, red chili, garam masala and salt
6. Mix well and cook for 2 minutes
7. Garnish with chopped cilantro
8. Enjoy as is in a bowl with toast or stuffed inside a tortilla or pita pocket

. . . .

Variations

Vary the vegetables per your preference in step 4
Top with sliced avocado for an additional luscious and creamy topping
Serve with a drizzle of green chutney or garlic chutney for an extra fiery kick

Indian Style Nachos

Papdi Chaat

An Indian version of Nachos with a sweet and tangy flavor profile

Chaat is the term used to describe a variety of food choices such as pani puri, bhel puri, dahi sev puri, aloo tikki and more. Papdi chaat has a wonderful explosion of textures and flavors from the crunchy papdi (chips) layered with beans, herbs, veggies, cooling yogurt, spicy green chutney and sweet date chutney.

Traditionally, papdi is made from refined white flour and deep fried. My version provides a healthier option without compromising on flavor.

Ingredients

Serves 4

- ✿ 4 whole grain tortilla or roti, cut into strips and baked
- ✿ 2 cups garbanzo beans (1 14-oz can drained and thoroughly rinsed)
- ✿ 1 cup potato (peeled, cooked and cut into small pieces)
- ✿ 1 cup yogurt preferably Greek or Icelandic style (you can swap this for a plant based option or skip this) - whisked to allow for easy layering
- ✿ ¼ cup green chutney
- ✿ ¼ cup pomegranate arils
- ✿ ¼ cup finely chopped cilantro

Method

Baked Papdi

1. Preheat oven to 350 degrees Fahrenheit
2. Brush oil or spray tortillas with nonstick cooking spray
3. Cut each tortilla into 8-12 wedges
4. Line a baking sheet with tortillas in a single layer - avoid overlapping
5. Bake for 8-12 minutes - may need to check and rotate the sheet for even baking
6. Chips are done when the edges are browning and crispy

Assemble your papdi chaat

7. Divide all the ingredients into 4
8. Arrange papdi in a single layer on 4 plates
9. Layer garbanzo beans, potato cubes, yogurt, green chutney, pomegranate arils and finally cilantro in that order
10. Serve and enjoy immediately as it will get soggy quickly

Papdi chaat is a perfect make-ahead meal that can be enjoyed on a warm summer night when you don't feel like turning on the stove. Prepare all the ingredients ahead of time so you can pull this together anytime.

Spicy Mixed Vegetables and Toasted Wheat Bread

Pav Bhaji

A popular street food dish which translates to pav - bread, bhaji - vegetables.

Delicious vegetables cooked in a tomato sauce infused with aromatic spices and enjoyed with bread. Traditionally, it is made with a lot of butter to offset some of the spice level and potatoes are the predominant vegetable used in this dish. My version below is loaded with veggies and healthier.

Ingredients

Serves 4

- ✿ 1 tablespoon oil
- ✿ 1.5 teaspoons minced garlic
- ✿ 4 cups riced vegetable medley (cauliflower, carrots, broccoli) or your choice of 4 cups of cooked vegetables (carrots, green beans, bell pepper, cauliflower work well)
- ✿ 2 medium-sized potatoes, cooked, peeled and chopped
- ✿ 1 14-oz diced tomato can
- ✿ 1 14-oz tomato sauce can
- ✿ ½ teaspoon ground coriander
- ✿ ½ teaspoon ground cumin
- ✿ ½ teaspoon ground red chili (optional)
- ✿ 2-3 teaspoons garam masala
- ✿ 1 teaspoon salt
- ✿ 1 tablespoon butter
- ✿ 1 tablespoon lime juice

Garnish

- ✿ 2-3 tablespoons finely chopped cilantro
- ✿ ½ cup finely chopped onions (optional)

Pav

- ✿ 4-8 Dinner rolls or bread slices of your choice
- ✿ Oil or butter to toast

Method

1. Heat oil in a kadai/wok on medium high
2. Add garlic and sauté for 1 minute (make sure that the garlic does not burn)
3. Add riced vegetables or cooked vegetables, potatoes, diced tomatoes, tomato sauce, coriander, cumin, red chili, garam masala, salt
4. Mix well, cover and cook for 5- 6 minutes (until all the vegetables are soft and cooked)
5. Add butter, mix well and turn off the stove
6. Add lime juice, mix well, top with cilantro and enjoy

Pav/Bread

Typically, this is a soft dinner roll that is buttered and pan toasted.
Feel free to serve with bread of your choice.
I like to use wholegrain toast

Curried Power Bowl

I have taken some of my favorite ingredients and created an easy one bowl meal for convenience, flavor and easy clean up. The golden hue of turmeric and aromatics turn each bite into a flavor and textural explosion. The addition of garbanzo beans to this recipe provides a nice protein and fiber upgrade. This recipe came about one warm summer day when I had just gotten home from work and wanted to relax in our backyard with my family. I pulled together a few ingredients that I thought may play well together and cooked this in a wok in our backyard stove while sipping on some wine. This dish is in honor of my husband who loves simple one-bowl meals.

Ingredients
Makes 4-6 servings

- 1 tablespoon oil
- 1 teaspoon cumin seeds
- 1 large onion, chopped ~1 1/3 cup
- 2 serrano chili (deseeded and chopped) optional
- ½ teaspoon ground red chili
- 1 teaspoon turmeric
- 1 teaspoon ground cumin
- 1 teaspoon ground coriander
- 1 teaspoon garam masala
- 1 teaspoon garlic
- 1 teaspoon ginger
- 8 cups cauliflower florets ~2 pounds (about 1-1.5 large heads)
- 2 14-oz cans garbanzo beans rinsed and drained
- 4 tomatoes chopped
- Bag of greens

Method

1. Heat oil on medium high setting in a saucepan
2. Add cumin seeds and sauté for ~1 minute until darker brown
3. Add onions and sauté until golden brown
4. Add red chili, turmeric, cumin, coriander, garam masala, garlic, ginger, sauté for 1 minute
5. Add cauliflower and mix well and cook for ~5 minutes
6. Add garbanzo beans, tomatoes, mix well, cover and cook for 5-7 minutes
7. Garnish with cilantro and enjoy

. . . .

Serving suggestions
1. Serve on a bed of greens with a drizzle of cucumber raita
2. Place it inside a whole grain tortilla and enjoy as a wrap
3. Enjoy with a side of quinoa or rice

Indulgent Desserts

Desserts and Sweets are not part of a typical family meal. Growing up, we would usually have fresh fruit for dessert. However, sweets are a big part of festivals, holidays and celebrations. In the North, you are often welcomed as a guest with something sweet or you begin the meal with a sweet treat. In the South, usually the sweet is served at the end of a meal. This dichotomy was fascinating to me when we would visit family in the north or have guests visit our home in the south. Indian desserts are usually prepared on the stove top and not baked in the oven.

Indulgent Desserts

Sweetened Wheat and Cardamom Dessert

Sheero

An easy and flavorful dessert that is very common in Gujarat, India. A typical North-Indian home would have all of the ingredients for this recipe on hand. This sweet holds a special place in my heart as it was the first recipe I learned from my Mom. I prepared it for my first time for a high school culinary contest and it was a big hit. I have modified the traditional recipe to cut back on the sugar and fat by half. My Mom's recipe was 1 cup each of the first 4 ingredients. I love making it for my family and passing this tradition down.

Ingredients

Makes 4 servings

- 1/2 cup Ghee (clarified butter can be found at Indian grocery stores) or your choice of plant based oil or shortening
- 1 cup Whole Wheat Flour
- 3/4 cup Water
- 1/2 cup Sugar
- 1 tablespoon ground cardamom

Method

1. Heat Ghee in a non-stick pan. Add whole wheat flour to melted ghee and keep stirring on medium heat for ~7-8 minutes until the color changes/darkens.
2. Add water and sugar simultaneously, turn stove down to low and keep stirring for ~3-5 minutes until all the sugar has dissolved.
3. Add cardamom, mix well, turn off the stove.
4. Serve immediately and enjoy it hot.

. . . .

Note

It is important to have all the ingredients measured and ready next to you before you start making the recipe
If you like nuts, you can add chopped nuts or slivered almonds as a garnish before serving
Sprinkle finely chopped fruit - berries, apples, or pomegranate arils for an added visual and textural pop

Vermicelli Milk Pudding

Payasam - A milk-based sweet porridge-like south Indian dessert

Semiya Payasam - a sweet milk porridge made with vermicelli

There are many variations of payasam, here is a simple one made with vermicelli. To make this plant based, simply swap the cow's milk for your plant based beverage of choice and use coconut oil instead of ghee.

Ingredients
Makes 4 servings
- 4 cups milk
- 1 tablespoon ghee
- 1 cup vermicelli or angel hair pasta broken into 1" length pieces
- ½ cup sugar
- ½ cup raw, cashew nuts broken into pieces
- 1 teaspoon ground cardamom

Method
1. Boil milk either in the microwave or in a separate pot
2. Heat 1 teaspoon ghee in a heavy pot on medium-high. Fry cashew pieces until golden brown and set aside
3. Heat remaining 2 teaspoons ghee in the same pot on medium and add vermicelli pieces. Fry until golden brown in color
4. Add boiling milk, sugar, mix well and continue to cook for 5 minutes
5. Reduce heat, simmer and stir frequently until the mixture has thickened to a creamy consistency
6. Add cardamom and mix well
7. Remove from heat and serve hot topped with fried cashews

This payasam can be served hot or cold as a delicious dessert

Garbanzo Fudge Balls

Magas

A delicious cardamom-flavored garbanzo flour dessert which can be served as balls called Ladoo or cut into square pieces. It has a luxurious and decadent mouth feel and is infused with an amazing cardamom flavor. When I was young, I remember visiting my aunt who served me magas as an after-school treat. I had just learned about mountains at school that day and insisted on calling magas "mountain" since it sort of looked like one. To this day, my cousins tease me about my special name for magas.

Ingredients

Makes 12 ladoos/balls

- ¼ cup ghee
- 1 cup garbanzo flour (besan)
- ½ cup powdered sugar
- 1 teaspoon ground cardamom

Method

1. Heat ghee in a large skillet over medium high
2. Add garbanzo flour and cook until it is fragrant and begins to darken in color while stirring regularly. This will take 7-10 minutes
3. Remove from pan and cool for two minutes
4. Add powdered sugar, cardamom and mix well
5. Spread a little ghee on your palms before picking up 1 tablespoon mixture at a time to press and roll into balls
6. If the mixture feels too dry and crumbles, add a little more melted ghee as needed
7. Enjoy the magas warm or store in an airtight container

I have many fond memories of my Mom making fresh magas as an after-school treat. I would climb up on the kitchen counter and watch her lovingly make me just one piece of magas.

Almond Cookies

Badam Puri

A delicious almond cookie-like dessert that comes together very quickly. Badam is the Indian name for almond. Almonds have been used in various ways in Indian cuisine for their taste but especially for their health benefits. Growing up in India, my parents always encouraged us to have at least 6-7 almonds every morning before school and especially before an exam. Almonds were promoted as helpful for memory and brain power. This recipe is gluten-free and can be made vegan by using a plant-based beverage (almond, soy, hemp).

Ingredients

Makes 12

- 1 cup almond meal
- ½ cup powdered sugar
- 1 teaspoon ground cardamom
- ½ teaspoon saffron
- 3 tablespoons milk or plant based dairy alternative

Method

1. Preheat oven to 375 degrees Fahrenheit.
2. Line a baking sheet with parchment paper and set aside
3. Mix almond meal, powdered sugar and ground cardamom together in a bowl
4. Microwave milk and saffron for 20-25 seconds in a small bowl
5. Add liquid to the dry ingredients and mix well to form a soft dough
6. Divide dough into 12 pieces
7. Roll and flatten each piece into discs
8. Place the discs on lined baking sheet and bake for 4-5 minutes in the oven, flip the discs and bake for another 4-5 minutes
9. Enjoy fresh while warm or place in an airtight container and enjoy later

Sweetened Rice and Lentils

Sakkarai Pongal

This is a traditional rice and lentil dish served as an offering to god and prepared especially for the South Indian festival Pongal. Pongal is celebrated in January and is a four day festival celebrating the harvest. I have made the recipe healthier while still retaining the flavor profile by increasing the dal (lentils) and cutting back on the ghee. I have also used brown sugar as it is readily available in your local stores instead of jaggery (found in Indian stores).

Ingredients

Makes 8 (½ cup servings)
- ½ cup long grain white rice
- ½ cup moong dal
- 3 cups water
- ⅓ cup brown sugar
- ½ teaspoon ground cardamom
- ¼ teaspoon ground nutmeg
- 1 teaspoon ghee or oil
- ¼ cup raw cashews, broken into pieces

Method

1. In a saucepan, dry roast rice and dal for 3-4 minutes on medium heat until fragrant
2. Rinse the toasted rice and dal in a sieve
3. Add the rinsed dal and rice back into the saucepan, add water and bring to a boil
4. Turn down the heat to low, cover and cook for 20-25 minutes (until rice and dal are soft and cooked)
5. Use a wooden spoon to lightly mash the rice and dal
6. Add brown sugar, spices, mix well and turn off the stove
7. In a small pan, heat ghee and roast cashew pieces until golden brown
8. Add the melted ghee and cashew pieces on top of the rice dal mixture
9. Enjoy

. . . .

Variations
You can add ¼ cup unsweetened shredded coconut flakes in step 8
You can add 2-4 tablespoons dried raisins to step 7 and 8

Cardamom Infused Fruit Salad

Elaichi Fruit Salad

A vibrant and colorful fruit salad infused with Indian spices that makes a refreshing ending or accompaniment to any meal. Elaichi is the Indian name for cardamom.

Ingredients

Serves 4

- 1 banana cut into wheels
- 1 apple, cored and cut into cubes
- 1 orange, peeled, segmented and cubed
- 1 cup berries
- ½ teaspoon ground cardamom
- 1 teaspoon freshly squeezed lime juice

Method

1. Place all the fruit pieces into a bowl
2. Add ground cardamom and lime juice
3. Mix well while being gentle
4. Serve immediately or cool and serve when ready as is or with a scoop of ice cream

....

Note

You can vary up the fruit according to what is in season and your preferences. Instead of cardamom, you could add ground ginger or chai masala. You can also make this spicy by adding ¼ tsp ground red chili and ¼ teaspoon ground cumin. Feel like some herbs, you can add finely chopped cilantro or mint to the fruit salad. You can also add this fruit salad to a bed of greens with some chopped nuts or seeds for a delicious light meal.

Coconut Fudge Balls

Coconut Ladoo

A quick and delicious coconut treat.

Ladoo is the term used for a ball shaped sweet treat. There are many types of ladoos served in India. Coconut is considered to be auspicious and used in various forms in Indian cooking as well as in religious ceremonies. Coconut ladoo is often served as part of a festive meal. When rolling the balls, add more coconut as needed to help them retain their shape.

Ingredients

Makes 8

- 1 cup shredded, unsweetened coconut + ¼ cup for final garnish
- ½ cup condensed milk
- 1 teaspoon ghee or coconut oil

Method

1. Set aside ¼ cup of shredded coconut on a plate
2. Place the shredded coconut in a skillet over low heat and roast for 2 minutes
3. Add condensed milk and mix well
4. When the mixture becomes thick, turn off the stove and let the mixture cool until easy to handle by hand
5. Divide mixture into 8 portions
6. Spread ghee or coconut oil on your palms, scoop one portion at a time, roll and mold into a ball
7. Roll the balls one at a time in the shredded coconut
8. Enjoy immediately or store in an airtight container in the refrigerator for later

Delicious Drinks

Depending upon the weather, hot beverages with warming spices or cool beverages are popular. Tea is the popular drink in North India and coffee is popular in the south. Milk and dairy play an important role in Indian kitchens. However, you can easily substitute your favorite plant based beverage for milk in the recipes.

Turmeric Milk Latte

Haldi Doodh

A warm and spiced beverage that is tasty and healthy. Haldi is the Hindi name for turmeric, doodh is the Hindi name for milk. Turmeric is known for its anti-inflammatory properties. When turmeric is enjoyed with black pepper, the compound piperine in black pepper enhances absorption of turmeric by almost a 1000 percent. Curcumin the key compound in turmeric with health benefits works best with a fat and when heated up. Growing up in India, turmeric was used in a variety of ways in cooking but also as a remedy for colds/cough. Traditionally, it was made with hot milk, turmeric powder, a pinch of salt and ghee to coat your throat. I really did not like the way it tasted and would avoid it at all costs. I have played around with the basic ingredients to create a beverage that I actually look forward to drinking even when I am not sick.

Ingredients

Makes 1 serving

- 1 cup milk or dairy alternative beverage
- ¾ teaspoon ground turmeric
- ½ teaspoon ground cinnamon
- ¼ teaspoon ground ginger
- A dash of freshly ground black pepper
- 1 teaspoon ghee or coconut oil
- 1 tablespoon honey or sweetener of your choice

Method

1. Pour milk, turmeric, cinnamon, ginger, and black pepper into a mug and microwave until hot ~90-120 seconds
2. Add ghee or coconut oil and honey. Mix well
3. Enjoy

Almond Milk

Badam Doodh

A festive almond milk that can be enjoyed warm or cold. Badam is the Hindi word for almonds, doodh is the Hindi word for milk

Ingredients

Serves 4

- ½ cup almond meal
- 4 cups milk or dairy alternative of your choice (separated into 3.5 cups and ½ cup)
- ½ teaspoon ground cardamom
- 4 teaspoons sugar or sweetener of your choice (optional)

Method

1. Blend almond meal and ½ cup milk to create a smooth paste. Set aside
2. Heat 3.5 cups milk in a saucepan on the stove until it starts to boil
3. Add almond paste and sugar. Mix well and continue to simmer for 2-3 minutes
4. Turn off the stove, add ground cardamom and mix well.
5. Pour into four cups and enjoy as is or place in refrigerator to enjoy cold at a later time

Traditionally, this recipe is made by soaking raw almonds in water for 4-5 hours, peeling the skin and then blending it into a paste. By using almond meal, I have made this a much quicker process. However, if you have the time and would like to do this from scratch, soak 48 almonds in water for 4-5 hours, remove the skin and crush with milk into a paste before proceeding with the rest of the recipe above.

Saffron and Cardamom Flavored Milk

Kesar Pista Elaichi Doodh

A saffron infused, comforting beverage

Kesar is the Hindi word for saffron, pista is the Hindi word for pistachios, elaichi is the Hindi word for cardamom, and doodh is the term for milk.

Ingredients

Serves 4
- 1 teaspoon saffron strands
- 2 tablespoons warm milk of your choice
- 4 cups milk of your choice
- 4 teaspoons sugar or sweetener of your choice (optional)
- 1 teaspoon ground cardamom
- 2-4 teaspoons finely chopped pistachios

Method

1. In a small bowl mix saffron strands and 2 tablespoons warm milk. Set aside
2. Heat 4 cups of milk in a saucepan on medium-high heat, stir occasionally and bring to a boil
3. Turn down the heat to low, add saffron-milk mixture, sugar, and cardamom
4. Mix well, turn off the stove
5. Pour into 4 cups, top off with finely chopped pistachios and enjoy

. . . .

Note

If you don't like crunchy nut pieces, you can omit the pistachios or blend them along with saffron-milk mixture before adding in step 3. Feel free to substitute the milk for a plant based beverage of your preference.

Mango Smoothie

Mango Lassi

Mango lassi is a delicious sweet and cooling beverage that compliments spicy Indian cuisine. Mango is the national fruit of India and there are so many varieties available throughout the Indian summer season. When you try a mango lassi at a restaurant, most likely it is made from sweetened mango pulp. This is quite different from making it at home with fresh or frozen mangos.

Ingredients

Serves 4

- ✿ 2 cups diced fresh or frozen mango
- ✿ 2 cups plain yogurt (preferably Greek or Icelandic as they are higher in protein)
- ✿ 1 cup cold milk or dairy alternative
- ✿ 2 tablespoons sugar (optional)

Method

1. Place all the ingredients in your blender and blend until a smooth pureed consistency
2. Divide into 4 glasses and enjoy

. . . .

Note

If you like your lassi colder, you can add ice cubes to the blender and crush along with fruit and milk

Fragrant Indian Spiced Tea

Masala Chai

A warm and delicious beverage made with black tea and aromatics. Chai refers to both the tea and the beverage Masala is the term used for spices. Every family has their own version of spices that go into their tea according to their preference. Growing up in South India, coffee was much more common. However, my family is originally from Gujarat (Northwestern State) known for masala chai. My mom would either pick individual spices to highlight or add a combination to create an intense but delicious flavor.

Ingredients

Serves 4

- ✿ 2.5 cups water
- ✿ 2 cups milk or dairy alternative
- ✿ 4 teaspoons black tea (loose) or tea bags
- ✿ ¾-1 teaspoon chai masala spice (from the basics section of this book)
- ✿ 2-4 teaspoons sugar or sweetener of your choice (optional)

Method

1. In a saucepan, heat water, milk, tea, spices on medium-high
2. Bring to a boil, turn down the heat to low and simmer for 10 seconds
3. Turn off the heat, strain the tea into four cups
4. Add sweetener of choice in each cup and serve

··

Variations

Add 6-8 fresh mint leaves in the final simmer - step 2

Add ½ teaspoon ground cardamom in the final simmer - step 2

Skip premade chai masala spices and add fresh, whole spices instead (1-1" cinnamon stick, 6 cloves, 4-6 green cardamom pods slightly smashed, 1 star anise, 4-6 black peppercorns)

Spicy Tomato Broth

Quick Tomato Rasam

Rasam is a broth based beverage prepared in a variety of ways. It is typically served with white rice on an almost daily basis in Madras. Growing up in India, this was my go-to choice when I was feeling under the weather. It is warm, comforting and clears out your sinuses with the spices. I have taken the key elements of rasam and created a quick almost instant version that is ready in 10 minutes.

Ingredients

Serves 4

- 1 cup tomato sauce (8 oz tomato sauce can)
- 4 cups water
- 1 teaspoon minced garlic
- ½ teaspoon minced ginger (optional)
- 2 teaspoons ground coriander
- 1 teaspoon ground cumin
- ½ teaspoon ground turmeric
- ½ teaspoon ground red chili (optional)
- ¼-½ teaspoon ground black pepper (optional)
- ½ teaspoon salt (adjust per your preference)
- 1.5 teaspoons ghee or oil
- 1 teaspoon cumin seeds
- ¼ teaspoon asafetida
- 2 tablespoons finely chopped cilantro

Method

1. Add tomato sauce, water, garlic, ginger, coriander, cumin, turmeric, red chili, black pepper, salt into a saucepan and bring to a slow boil on medium heat
2. In a small skillet or pan, heat ghee or oil, add cumin seeds and asafetida. Sauté for 15-30 seconds until cumin seeds have turned a darker brown
3. Add the ghee with seeds to the saucepan. Turn off the stove.
4. Serve into bowls or cups with garnish of cilantro and enjoy

....

Note

Omit or increase the amount of red chili and black pepper according to your spice level preference

Best to bring rasam to a slow boil on medium low or low heat. It is important to turn off the stove as soon as the rasam comes to a boil. Keep your rasam saucepan covered until you are ready to enjoy it to maintain the aroma.

A Few Meal Ideas

1. Plain White Rice or Brown Rice Pulav, Rajma, plain yogurt
2. Roti or Puri with Chana Masala and Kachumber
3. Lemon rice with Sundal and Cucumber Raita
4. Coconut rice with Keerai Kootu
5. Plain Rice, Sambar and Green Bean Poriyal
6. Roti, Eggplant and Green Pea stir-fry, and Masoor Dal
7. Khichdi, Zucchini Tomato Curry and Plain Yogurt
8. Khaman Dhokla with Green Chutney and Masala Chai

Easy Meals Formula

- ☼ Pick a bean or lentil
- ☼ Pick a vibrant veggie
- ☼ Pick a grain (if you don't have time to make this - enjoy your meal with a whole grain tortilla or store-bought frozen brown rice or quinoa)
- ☼ If it is a special meal and you have the time, add a dessert/sweet or beverage

Feel free to mix and match recipes in this book. It does not have to be a completely Indian meal for you to enjoy these recipes. For example, you can enjoy any of the vibrant vegetables or rice dishes as sides to your protein option. Enjoy any of the beans or lentils section (except the sprouted bean salad) as a stew or soup. Try the delicious accompaniments with a charcuterie platter or inside your sandwiches.

Eat Well Your Way for Life Food Philosophy

When it comes to food, love for cooking and sharing the joy, my mother had a profound impact on my life. I use her wisdom as well as my science-based education as a dietitian to leave you with these thoughts.

1. Prepare food with a loving mindset as it permeates into your food.
2. Food prepared with a joyous attitude will help those eating it to feel good and thrive
3. Be thankful for the blessings of good food and company
4. Sit down when eating and take your time savoring the meal
5. Pay attention to ingredients and select them carefully
6. When able, take time to plan your meals and shop accordingly
7. Be creative with leftovers so you minimize wastage and maximize flavor
8. It is okay to take shortcuts
9. There is great joy in preparing food and seeing others enjoy it
10. Always be open and receptive to learning
11. Food is so much more than fuel for your body
12. Regardless of how busy you are, taking a few minutes to gather around a table with delicious food can be rejuvenating and fun

Cheers and Namaste

References

Dalal, Tarla. *The Complete Gujarati Cookbook* (2002). 5th Printing. Mumbai, India: Sanjay & Company.

Giri, J. (2013). *Cooking at home with pedatha: Best vegetarian book in the world - gourmand winner*. Chennai, India: Wisdom Tree.

Jaffrey, Madhur.(1988). *A Taste of India*. New York: Atheneum

Larson Duyff, R. (2017), *Academy of Nutrition and Dietetics Complete Food & Nutrition guide*. 5th edition. New York, NY:Houghton Mifflin Harcourt Publishing Company

Misra, R. (2011). *Indian foods: AAPIs guide to nutrition, health and diabetes*. New Delhi: Allied.

Norman, Jill. (1995). *The Complete Book of Spices: A Practical Guide to Spices and Aromatic Seeds*. New York: Penguin Books

Patil, Vimla. *A Cook's Tour of South India*. New Delhi: Sterling Publishers Private Limited, 1998.

Winfrey, Oprah. (2017), *Food Health and Happiness*. New York, NY. Melcher Media.

www.eatright.org

Index

About the Author

Vandana Sheth, RDN, CDE, FAND, is the owner of a nutrition consulting practice focusing on diabetes, eating disorders, food allergies, health promotion and disease prevention. She has over two decades of experience working with individuals, groups, community organizations and schools and specializes in intuitive eating, food allergies, vegetarian nutrition, diabetes and family nutrition. She has written numerous articles on nutrition for magazines and other professional publications and has served as a nutrition expert specializing in food allergies and vegetarian nutrition with a multitude of community organizations. As a National Spokesperson for the Academy of Nutrition and Dietetics, representing one of the largest media markets, Vandana frequently speaks to a wide range of audiences on hot topics related to health, wellness, nutrition and disease prevention. She provides dynamic presentations including vegetarian cooking demonstrations to promote a healthy lifestyle. Vandana has done countless media interviews and is frequently quoted in print publications as well as online media. Some examples of her media appearances/quotes include: Huffington Post, Self Magazine, Diabetes Today, Diabetes Living, Today's Dietitian, Ladies Home Journal, Time, Chicago Tribune, Los Angeles Times, San Diego Tribune, Weight Watchers, Prevention, Shape, US weekly, US News & World report, Washington Post, WebMD, Kidseatright, EverydayHealth, Men's Health, CBS, and Torrance Citicable. She was honored to receive the 2016 Excellence in Private Practice, Business and Communications award by the California Academy of Nutrition and Dietetics.

Vandana's love for gathering around a table with delicious, home-cooked meals began as a child watching her mother, who so lovingly and creatively wove her kindness and open heart into every meal, pulling people in from the community to their family table and celebrations. Vandana now carries on this tradition through her own love for spending quality time with family and friends, watching American football, traveling, enjoying fine dining and wine tasting experiences and long walks with their dog, Shadow. *My Indian Table* is Vandana's first cookbook; one of many to come in the future.

Vandana provides in-person counseling sessions in her Torrance office, as well as virtual health coaching sessions to clients nationwide.

Contact her at www.vandanasheth.com for more information as well as to invite her for speaking engagements.

Vandana would love to hear from you and is active on social media.

You can find her on

 @vandanashethRDCDE

 @vandanashethrd

 @vandanasheth

Made in the USA
Las Vegas, NV
16 February 2023

67655411R00090